Don't Ever Give Up on Love

True Stories of Senior Romances

Timothy Carroll

iUniverse, Inc.
Bloomington

iUniverse books may be ordered through booksellers or by contacting:

iUniverse
1663 Liberty Drive
Bloomington, IN 47403
www.iuniverse.com
1-800-Authors (1-800-288-4677)

Because of the dynamic nature of the Internet, any web addresses or links contained in this book may have changed since publication and may no longer be valid. The views expressed in this work are solely those of the author and do not necessarily reflect the views of the publisher, and the publisher hereby disclaims any responsibility for them.

Any people depicted in stock imagery provided by Thinkstock are models, and such images are being used for illustrative purposes only.

Certain stock imagery © Thinkstock.

ISBN: 978-1-4502-9259-7 (sc)
ISBN: 978-1-4502-9260-3 (hc)
ISBN: 978-1-4502-9261-0 (ebook)

Printed in the United States of America

Library of Congress Control Number: 2011901156

iUniverse rev. date: 03/16/2011

I dedicate this book to the one I love - Yvonne

Acknowledgements

I wish to acknowledge with gratitude the contributions to the stories in this book from the following people:-

Barbara Bicknell and John Goodwin

Gina Bouchard and Gary Tissue

Cecilia Branhut

Linda and Charles Cattanach

Marianne and John Curtin

Neely and Ron Denney

Toni and Jerry Dore

Nicki and Ronnie Herman

Lou and Bill Holton

Lois Hoopes and Sam Focer

Ginny Montgomery

Judy and Bob Moreno

Susan and Bill Pearce

Winnie Roote and Michael Habicht

Mary Copes and Jerry Sanders

Eleanor and Bill Stubba

Barbara Wastart and Duane Thoresen

Preface—A Fairy Tale

The love we give away is the only love we keep.

—Elbert Hubbard

Once upon a time, a beautiful maturing princess finally lost her beloved prince to cancer after a prolonged illness. Her children and her grandchildren were supportive and tried to console her. Nevertheless, she was sad and often felt alone.

For many months, which gradually became years, all she did almost every day was stay at home reading and listlessly watching TV. She often slept late in the mornings, losing half the day because time didn't seem to matter anymore. She enjoyed her family, as she had always done, but there was a big gap in her life that she didn't really want to fill, even if she had known how. Her children helped her a lot by taking her away with them on holidays and cruises with their families, but they also had their own busy lives to live, and she could only be with them some of the time. She lacked the company of people her own age.

Then one day, a former colleague remembered that she was alone and asked a sociable friend to call her. This friend was more like a fairy godmother who waved a magic wand because, before she knew it, she was meeting many other people for the first time—all through this sociable friend.

She met men as well as women, but she didn't feel ready to form a romantic relationship. She just enjoyed, on neutral territory, the regular company of friendly contemporaries who had also found themselves on their own for one reason or another.

For two or more years, she developed a new life among this active group of friends. There were parties to organize, dances to arrange, outings and trips, and always special friends for company. Suddenly, she noticed that there was no longer a gap in her life at all, and it seemed as though the sadness was lifting from her. She still held close her fond memories of her dear departed prince, but now she could focus on new interests and find herself worthy, loving, and valued by others. She thought that perhaps she could live like this happily ever after.

Once upon a time, there was a fine prince who traveled far and created many enterprises over many years. However, there came a time in a far-off land when his fortunes changed and disaster struck him. He found himself abandoned by those he loved and by some of his friends as well. So he began a new adventure and a new enterprise, which took him, by chance, across the ocean to the land where the beautiful princess lived.

For many years, he lived far away, until he finally sought a change and moved to the very city where she happened to live. He was not looking for a romantic attachment. He socialized because it was part of his business networking activity. One day he met a friendly man at one such event, and he was invited to come and meet a group to which he belonged. In due course, the prince accepted this invitation. It was then that the prince met the princess for the first time. Over the next few months, through meeting among the same group and joining its activities, they became friends and soon fell head over heels in love with each other. The prince proposed, the princess accepted, and they were married eight months later, living happily ever after.

This may sound a little like a fairy tale—but it is in fact a true story. There are probably many more just like it. It can often seem as though love and happiness find you when you are not really looking for them, for sometimes the harder you seek them, the more elusive they become.

So what is the answer? It is certainly not to wait around at home for love. Who even knows or cares that you are there? At the same time, it is also important for your own self-esteem and self-respect not to go out pursuing romance too hard, even though you may be successful at it. Good friendships and lasting relationships often stem from enjoyment or engagement in common activities. So pursuing what interests and amuses you is a good starting point as long as it takes you out to where other people live, work, and play.

Contents

Part One

Introduction

Chapter One—The Courage to Date Again

Love doesn't make the world go 'round; love is what makes the ride worthwhile.

—Franklin P. Jones

It would be nice, wouldn't it, if the people who sought us out during our busy youths would miraculously reappear when we are lonely and older?

Surely many of you women can remember dating men when you were at college. There were social mixers, fraternity parties, and dances. Friends and friends of friends, or even parents, would fix you up. You had some connection, however tenuous, with the men you dated. You were rarely in the company of a total stranger. It was different then because most of us lived at home when we were not at college. We were largely living in a protected, supportive, and familiar place.

A girl was typically expected to return home from college with a husband or at least a prospective husband in mind. Outside the college environment, many who are grandmothers today were married by the age of sixteen or seventeen. There was even a social stigma in being "left on the shelf". No girls wished to disappoint their parents or families by remaining single beyond their mid-twenties. For the majority, great importance was attached to establishing a family as soon as possible. The well-being of young women was quickly placed in the hands of their young husbands.

Now that more than twenty or thirty years have elapsed, our expectations of romantic partners in our lives are different. Our desires for such relationships have grown out of more than half a century of living experience. Our goals have changed. We have grown up, hopefully gained some wisdom, and become more comfortable with ourselves. If we are even ready to approach the concept of dating again, it is with a different attitude.

When we were young and broke up with a girlfriend or boyfriend, getting over it, in most cases, lasted about as long as it took to find a replacement. However, after many years of marriage, and after experiencing the loss of a loved one through divorce or death, it may take years to recover. It is therefore important to complete the healing process and feel good about oneself before launching into a new social life. It would be unfair to work out one's temporary adjustment on someone new and innocent, someone who may have genuine feelings for you and long-term expectations.

Overall, when contemplating the second or third time around, the focus of a relationship shifts away from establishing a family and moves toward companionship, intimacy, sharing, caring, and security. Of course, we want the positive ingredients of humor, love, romance, and good times, but we may be more inclined to choose a partner, companion, or spouse based on mutual interests.

The prospect of dating again can be quite daunting at first. Conventions have changed. We are out of date. It is confusing. There is, as always, the possibility of rejection. We have lost the bloom of youth and may have gained more weight than we would have liked; we may also feel that we have become rather set in our ways. It has been so long since we were on our own, and we are more than a little shy. Having lost once, we may fear losing again. Can we cope with the disappointment?

What about sex? Women and men who have been accustomed to the same sexual partner for many years may feel anxious about going to bed with a stranger. And imagine a girl's former college sweetheart returning in later years to become her boyfriend. He is familiar and close but still a comparative stranger to her body. Then there is the matter of how well our body parts still function. Is our libido sufficiently strong? Certainly one's sex drive tends to diminish with advancing years, but for men, the introduction of drugs such as Viagra can help maintain active sexual relationships. They can also lead to excessive promiscuity. It is claimed that sexually transmitted diseases among older people have increased at the fastest rate on record. It is a matter of behaving responsibly and taking the necessary precautions.

Regardless of age, consensual sex is good and forms the intimate cornerstone of most romantic relationships. It not only excites and thrills its participants, but it also confirms their oneness, their togetherness, the two halves of their single whole. It establishes the essential bond of mutual trust and exclusivity that makes each partner feel complete in the presence of the other.

As we mature, we appreciate the comfort and the value of simply being hugged and touched tenderly by someone we admire. It may have no sensual connotation at all, but it can create much warmth, energy, and a feeling of worthiness.

People have said that lust can kill, whereas love never can. Lust is a self-gratifying drive that can sometimes be mistaken for love when it occurs simultaneously in people who are attracted to each other. Love, on the other hand, is a more unselfish emotion that places its object on a higher level of importance than one's own.

- **Beware of Misunderstandings**

Daphne became frustrated by a recent blind date. She met him at a popular venue, where they talked over a couple of drinks and then danced together for a while. He was a pleasant man, and Daphne, who had not been out with a man in quite a while, appreciated his company. She had baked some cookies during the afternoon and thought he might like one. So as they were about to bid each other farewell, she invited him back to her house for coffee. She had been used to having people visit her at home while she was married and didn't really think anything of it when she invited her date to do the same. When he was leaving, however, he mentioned that he had learned that when a woman invites a man home "for coffee" it means that she wants to go to bed with him. Daphne was horrified.

It actually takes a lot more attitude and signaling for such an innocent invitation to be interpreted in this way, and this was probably just a guy trying to get a reaction.

- **When you least expect it**

In another example, Barbara was married several times before she moved from California to Florida. She had originally immigrated to America from England, where she had worked for British Airways and subsequently for TWA. She was still with TWA when she was invited to move to America permanently. She was quickly promoted to senior management. However, other interesting opportunities lay ahead.

In Florida, Barbara became a commercial real estate broker. Romantic relationships occurred while she pursued her busy and challenging career. However, there came a time when she found herself tiring of her second try with the same joyful but feckless boyfriend.

She had lost interest in men altogether by the time the affair ended. She is a generous and helpful woman whose kindness and success had been abused. Some men had tried to take advantage of her. Consequently, her ideas about relationships had become jaded. Yet she remained optimistic, cheerful, helpful, and shrewd.

She was friendly with a woman from Bosnia, named Halida, who owned a dress shop that she visited from time to time. It was located near her home at Sunset Beach.

Halida told Barbara about a male friend of hers who had recently been divorced. She described John as a good man who was steady and reliable. Barbara was in no mood for a blind date, and apparently, John had not expressed any interest in meeting her either.

One day, while Barbara was in the shop browsing the selection of dresses, Halida secretly telephoned John on his cell phone and tricked him into coming to the shop on the pretext of helping her fix a leak in her roof.

Being the good friend that he was, he immediately went home and changed into some work clothes, put his tools in his truck, and drove straight to Halida's shop. It was a testament to his promptness that, surprisingly, Barbara was still there.

Halida then sat John and Barbara down on a bench and served them tea and coffee as she normally did for her customers. She made the introductions and then suggested that John return home to change so that they could all go out to dinner together right away. Then they would be able get to know each other better

They met for a couple of dates after that. At that time, there was not much interest on Barbara's part, even though John was keen to pursue their friendship. She decided to take a trip to Copper Canyon in Mexico with a female friend who was a travel agent. Barbara's attitude toward men in general had softened very little. She was looking forward to some reliable female companionship.

The trip did not go as well as she had expected. Her companion turned out to be a difficult traveling partner. She was always complaining and was frequently late for the bus. Yet others blamed Barbara for this behavior because she shared the same room.

John had foreseen that Mexico might be short on snacks for the journey, so he had taken the trouble to give Barbara a liberal supply of candy and nuts beforehand. When the trip and its frustrations were over, Barbara landed at the airport in the United States to find John meeting her with a dozen roses. The relief in seeing him after such an awful week away convinced her that he was the right man for her after all.

Some six years later, having pooled their resources, they are still happily sharing each other's lives in a beautiful lakeside home in Florida. They run a lucrative business together and own a beachfront property in New Zealand, where they spend several months a year. All they ever needed was the courage to date again.

Chapter Two—It's Okay to Be Single

The best feelings are those that have no words to describe them.

—Michelle Hammersley

We should remember that as we go through life, through relationships, through marriage, children's upbringing, divorce, and bereavement, we are growing as people and developing. We are not always growing wiser, more intelligent, more beautiful, or happier, but we are certainly growing older and more experienced.

What does experience teach us? It varies from one individual to another, doesn't it? It may depend on what we are willing to learn. Sometimes we are sheltered or thwarted from knowing ourselves and our capabilities by the very nature of our lives and the people with whom we interact. Many of us simply become what we believe we are supposed to be. We become the grown-up, the wife, the husband, the mom, the dad, the breadwinner, or the boss. We become what life expects of us in the role that we have adopted to play. Who are we really, though?

When we find ourselves single in later life, for whatever reason, we should be able to revel in that fact—not disparage it. There is nothing to be ashamed of in being single. It allows us the freedom to know and love ourselves for who we truly are. It is a wonderful state with overwhelming possibilities. It also permits us to follow any course that we may choose. We can explore. We can travel. We can do something we love instead of something we have to do. Above all, we are able to engage in a variety of new relationships and friendships. They need not necessarily involve long-term commitments. They can be developed from the perspective of experience and devotion to our personal growth, which may not have been acceptable or possible before.

"I love men and animals," said Cecilia, "but not necessarily in that order." In reality, Cecilia loves life passionately. That includes all humanity. She is a mature, attractive, eloquent lady with a wide range of intellectual interests and activities. Playing tennis with great enthusiasm at least twice a week has kept her in good physical shape. She has a direct manner, an impish sense of humor, and particularly enjoys the freedom, contentment, and personal space that a single life provides. When so many people crave the companionship of a live-in partner, what brought Cecilia to this happy alternative?

Isobel Cecilia Rostkowsky, the daughter of a Russian Jewish father and a mother whose parents were Polish Jewish immigrants, grew up in the north London suburb of Highgate. Her father died from pancreatic cancer when she was only fourteen years of age. She was then attending Henrietta Barnett, a girls' school in Hampstead Garden Suburb, where she won awards for her writing and performing skills. She nursed a secret desire to pursue acting, not daring to share that with anyone, especially her mother.

When she left Henrietta Barnett, she allowed herself to be enrolled at the French Institute for a two-year bilingual business course. She remembers how sad her English teacher, Mrs. Fayers, looked when she heard of the plan. To this day, she wishes she had plucked up the courage to ask why.

While at the French Institute, Cecilia joined Unity Theatre. Because of the opportunity to rehearse and perform at Unity, she was able to tolerate the French Institute. Finally, the two dreary years ended, with the principal writing across her final report, *"Un gaspillage de temps,"* meaning "a waste of time." However, she was immediately able to get a job as a bilingual secretary with a Russian-owned company in the city. While there, she was still with Unity Theatre and took two weeks off to go with them to perform in Warsaw. The entire experience made a profound impression on her: the train ride through Belgium, Germany, Czechoslovakia, and of course, Poland—and also the detour to Auschwitz on their return.

Cecilia decided that to become professional, she should attend an accredited drama school. She went to Webber Douglas, a well-known school in London. To this day, she is not sure it was a good idea, even though, upon graduation, she was immediately accepted for a role at the Theatre Royal in Windsor. That was followed by a brief stint at Guildford Repertory Company as assistant stage manager. She also appeared in minor roles. This was frequently how young actors got started at that time. She still has a vinyl record of her singing, heard over the radio in one of the Guildford plays. She remembers being hunted down at a movie matinee to take over a major role that same evening. She did well.

That wasn't enough for the Guildford manager. She wanted more work and reminded him of her successes: "Don't you remember my singing and my famous last-minute saving of that evening performance?" He didn't care. She returned to London to do some TV and film work. She found rejection distasteful and was beginning to think that perhaps her future lay elsewhere.

Fate took Cecilia to a party where she met Joan Naismith, a woman who was sailing to New York in the New Year. The idea excited her so much that she immediately asked if she could tag along. Her life was about to change forever.

Before she left England, fate stepped in again when she went to another party. There she met Jonathan Bauer, a handsome young Jewish architectural student. They spent a glorious week together. Then off she and Joan sailed to New York, leaving her romantic inclinations behind with Jonathan, two years her junior. Her fantasies, by which she lived, included a suitor at least two years older. That's how it always was in novels by Jane Austen, Emily Brontë, and the others that she devoured.

Joan and Cecilia arrived in New York on January 20, 1961, to find deep snow. It was the day of President Kennedy's inauguration. Her intention was to find work and stay for just a year. She relished missing Jonathan, his missing her, and their loving letters back and forth across the Atlantic. His letters always began, "My darling Cecilia." She has them still, reminders of her misbehavior, immaturity, and what might have been.

A year later she returned to England for two weeks on vacation from her secretarial work in the office of Gobaud De Paris, a string of Manhattan cosmetic shops. Jonathan was waiting at the airport to meet her. Having settled so well in New York, she had no real intention of remaining in England quite yet. She wanted to return to New York to tie up loose ends, as she told her mother. She had no idea what she meant by that. Her mother liked Jonathan, and his parents liked Cecilia. How perfect it all was going to be!

How romantic it felt to ache for Jonathan on her flight back to New York. She had a vague idea of returning to London at some misty time in the future. However, Jonathan's attraction to her proved to be so strong that he decided to come to New York to be with her.

"That wasn't how I wanted the story to go," Cecilia said later. "He was to wait in London for me, and I was to long for him over the miles."

Therefore, once they were both in New York, his proximity did not sit well with Cecilia. She pushed him away and wanted nothing more to do with him. He was part of another life, which she might have recaptured in her own time and on her own terms. Her mother never showed her disappointment, but before she died in 1970, she did show considerable insight when she said to Cecilia, "Did Jonathan love you too much?"

She learned many years later that he met and married an American woman who followed him back to London, gave him two children, and enjoyed with him, possibly to this day, his success as an architect.

Meanwhile, life blossomed for Cecilia. She had long before adopted the stage name of Cecilia Ross, and she continued to use it in her new life. With the world at her feet, she had a wonderful time—full of fun and romance. There were many relationships, but none of them were permanent. Looking back on that time, she now feels that perhaps she tended to be more in lust than in love. She felt that once the initial passion and excitement had given way to the more mundane commitment of continued loving companionship, the relationship became stifling and an encumbrance to her.

Her reckless love life and inconstancy reached a point that caused her friend Miriam Chall to become concerned about her psychological state of mind. She recommended therapy—such a New York thing to do! Eventually, Cecilia landed in the Central Park West office of Abe Weinberg, MD, a psychiatrist. He began to treat Cecilia, and the results were superb.

By this time, she was enjoying a new career at an advertising agency in Times Square. They appreciated her ability and gave her exciting opportunities as an assistant account executive. On winter weekends, she skied in Vermont, and on summer weekends, she went to Fire Island. The new Cecilia, thanks to Honest Abe, her pet name for Dr. Weinberg, was able to work toward a more normal life.

Through Lee Katz, a friend and coworker, she met Bernie Branhut during a visit to Detroit. He was a good-looking divorced man in his mid-thirties. He and Cecilia carried on a brief long-distance relationship which, maybe for that very reason, proved to last longer than usual.

It was Dr Abe Weinberg who persuaded Cecilia that her problems would be solved by settling down and marrying. Why not Bernie Branhut?

"But I'm not sure he's the right man for me," said Cecilia.

"Shut up and get married," were Dr. Weinberg's exact words.

By then, she had developed enough confidence in him to believe that he might be right. So in September 1971, she and Bernie were married. The ceremony took place at a temple in Detroit, in the presence of a few friends. Bernie's stepfather, a true business tycoon— or, as Cecilia called him, a "typhoon"—paid for the reception.

A shocking event marred Cecilia's wedding. Bernie had two young daughters by his first wife, Linda, who had remarried her first husband. At that time, the little girls were only four and six years old and living with their mother. Five days before Cecilia and Bernie's marriage, Linda, alone with the girls, went upstairs and shot herself with her husband's hunting rifle. No one really understood why. She was a beautiful yet troubled woman and may have had a sudden urge to escape her demons.

It was then that Cecilia and Bernie decided that his daughters should come and live with them. Bernie said he was afraid that taking on the girls' upbringing might destroy their marriage, but Cecilia is convinced that it only lasted as long as it did because of them. Sadly, and despite Dr. Abe Weinberg's advice, Cecilia was never in love with Bernie, and the marriage was unlikely to succeed. However, thanks to the good relationship between Cecilia and Bernie's daughters, Lori and Sherri, it lasted seven years, much longer than Cecilia's average relationships. Ironically, Linda's mother, grandmother to Lori and Sherri, became a good friend of Cecilia's and remained so until her death.

"I'm not really happy," said Cecilia to Dr. Weinberg during a visit to New York.

"So get a divorce," was his terse reply.

Maybe it sounded frivolous and unprofessional, but he certainly had a point. After the divorce, Cecilia reveled in her freedom, hardly regretting that Bernie retained custody of Lori and Sherri. She returned to the world of advertising, first as copywriter at a small agency and then as account executive at Thompson Recruitment Advertising.

She commuted to Toronto one winter as acting branch manager of that office, flying out of Detroit Metro every Monday morning and returning every Friday evening. The bigwigs in the California headquarters had wanted her to relocate to Toronto, but she wasn't yet a citizen and might have lost her United States residency if she moved away. Eventually, they found someone else to take over the Toronto office, and Cecilia was happy to stay in America.

One day in 1986, while still at Thompson, she applied for a promotion to account director of the Northern Telecom account. It meant moving to Atlanta, but she didn't mind at all. However, after a brief relationship with Northern Telecom, they decided they didn't like Cecilia, and she didn't like them.

"Come back to Detroit," suggested the manager of that office. She flew up to talk to him about it. Wonderful as it was to see him and her old colleagues, she decided that she couldn't face Detroit's brutal winters again. She would stay in Atlanta and see what the future held.

It has been good. She has concluded that she is happier remaining single. She has many friends, men and women alike, and admirers too. Life continues much as it did before she was married. Some needs have diminished, and life on her own allows her an unprecedented level of stability, independence, contentment, and promise. She can enjoy her own space without intrusion and can follow a much wider selection of interests than if she were restricted by the demands of a romantic partnership.

She says, "As much as I love them, I wouldn't even share my space with a cat."

She has also developed a wider range of friends than would otherwise have been possible. For Cecilia it is the perfect balance—the ultimate status quo.

Some single people may hanker for a state of matrimony—even admiring it or envying it in others—but in the final analysis, they may be unwilling or too self-sufficient to embrace it. Of course, where there is a romantic factor, and a loving purpose in enhancing the life of another as well as one's own, then there is every hope that a closer bond will follow. However, there is still no reason why remaining single may not be the best state for certain individuals, and it is quite okay. The energy of single people can often be directed toward the community as a whole or groups within it. In this way, they embrace a larger or extended family. Is it perhaps better to be single and content than married and miserable?

When all is said and done, it is quite okay to be single.

Chapter Three—I Want to be Married, But …

We can only learn to love by loving.

—Iris Murdoch

In current society, over half of all marriages fail for one reason or another. So it is not surprising that people have become nervous about making commitments. It sometimes seems as though they stop trying when their relationships face challenges. Dating has become more like a race to try out as many people as possible rather than take enough time to get to know one person at a deeper level. Divorce is the equal resource of both men and women. It doesn't seem to matter whether a marriage has lasted thirty years or thirty months—the outcome is much the same.

Many potential marriages between mature adults have been sabotaged by angry children of former marriages because they cannot accept such change and resent it bitterly. As people mature, they sometimes gain a sense of who they are through their accumulated possessions, their position in society, or what they do for a living. A new romantic relationship—if pursued until marriage—can influence these factors in ways that require too much sacrifice. This can be seen as an invasion—requiring one to give up autonomy and identity.

Relationships require effort. They don't always run smoothly, and it takes a determined commitment from both partners to make one a success. Sometimes they break up for no other reason than, as the song goes, "love has died on the vine." That essential spark has gone, leaving both people feeling unfulfilled or inadequate. Despite the poor odds, however, long-lasting, healthy relationships are possible, as many have proved. What is the secret? Perhaps they made up their minds to cherish one another instead of relying too heavily on the warm, fuzzy feelings they had when they fell in love; this can ultimately develop into something stronger and deeper when allowed. If you have made that conscious choice, it is harder to break that promise you have made to yourself as well as your partner, and you are more inclined to weather the storms.

Jack was happily married to his second wife, Abby, for several years. He worked hard and had great energy and enthusiasm. He was well paid as a regional manager, beginning each day extremely early. Abby did part-time office work. When they were not working, they improved their home near the beach, played tennis, and socialized with their many friends. They were popular people. He was capable, charming, and personable, and she was intelligent, attractive, and eloquent. Their socializing usually involved drinking, as it does for most people. In Abby's case, though, it led to an addiction to wine. For a while, it seemed to be under control. As the years passed, however, it turned Abby, who was already clever, into a secretive, thieving, manipulating addict who was incapable of stopping. It took on the astounding proportions of a mental illness.

It began to impinge heavily on their relationship. He would return from work not knowing where Abby was, and she did not remember either. In order to bring her home, he would have to cruise all the bars where she might be found. Sometimes her car would be lodged against a tree with the engine still running, the driver's door open, and Abby collapsed and unconscious at the roadside. People would telephone him at night to report that they had seen a woman lying drunk in the surf on the beach, fully clothed with dogs sniffing around her, and wondered if it was his wife. On all these occasions, it fell to Jack to drag her home, undress her, and put her to bed. There were fights, streams of insults, and invective. Abby could be extremely vicious and vindictive when she had been drinking. Yet when she was sober, she could remember nothing of these incidents and became the affectionate, agreeable wife he recognized once again.

So life continued, from one day's crisis to another. After two years Jack finally asked Abby for a divorce. They agreed to sell their marital home and divide the proceeds. She wished to continue living in the same neighborhood. So Jack agreed to a generous settlement, which included payment for her admission to an expensive rehab clinic in another state and a long lease on a cottage in their old neighborhood, containing all her favorite pieces of their furniture, which she could return to after she was discharged.

Meanwhile, Jack bought a small one-level single family home in another town. His intention was to remodel and enlarge it. During Abby's addiction, they had lost touch with their former friends, and Abby's family had distanced themselves from her. Now that he was single, Jack started to seek a better social life and meet new friends. It began quite well. He made friends with the neighbors living on his street. Through subcontractors, he extended his new home and remodeled its interior in a most imaginative and contemporary style. It was the envy of all who saw it. He joined a tennis club again and other groups as well. He played golf and was invited to meetings, dinners, and parties.

There was no particular romantic involvement, and Jack continued to monitor Abby's progress at the rehab clinic. Although they were now divorced, he felt guilty about Abby, his treatment of her over her addiction, and the way things had ended between them. While he could not bear living with her while she was an alcoholic—her addiction ruined his life as well as her own—he still loved her and wished to help her recover.

She became suspicious that he was interested in a relationship with another woman and managed to manipulate an early discharge from the rehab clinic. She even borrowed her airfare from the head of the institution by charming him and convincing him that she was cured. She turned up in a taxi at the door of Jack's beautiful new home, not at the cottage that awaited her with all her things. She called him on a cell phone while he was shopping at the local grocery store and asked him to hurry home to pay her taxi fare. She had stolen wine, and she was intoxicated once again. An argument ensued, but she refused to leave or to return to the clinic. When he returned from work the next day, he discovered that she had not only been drinking heavily again, but that she had defecated on his new bed and throughout the house, broken his objets d'art, and destroyed some of his paintings. It seemed to be payback for the suspected presence of another woman, whether it was true or false. He persuaded her to go to her cottage by agreeing to give her some of his furniture that she particularly admired. He had to burn the sheets and new bedding that she had purposely soiled.

That is when the harassment began. She called him constantly, at work and at home and on his cell phone, accusing him of having a relationship with another woman, even though he was now quite entitled to do so. The calls became so intrusive that Jack finally obtained a restraining order against her. It was effective for a while.

Abby was actually hired to work for a law office. She was an impressive woman in an interview—confident, educated, well-spoken, and competent. Unfortunately, it was just one of many jobs that she lost shortly afterward due to intoxication and absenteeism.

When she eventually violated the restraining order Jack had obtained, she was arrested and sentenced to eighteen months in a federal rehab unit. Jack was able to continue his life unencumbered in the meantime, but the feelings of guilt persisted.

After a year of good behavior and sobriety, the authorities agreed that Abby could leave her facility to find daytime work, provided she returned to the facility at night. As her friends and family had abandoned her, the judge, rather surprisingly, asked Jack if he would be the person responsible for visiting her and monitoring her release for work.

Inevitably, he felt sorry for her and began to believe that she had truly recovered from her alcohol addiction. After all, she had remained perfectly sober while institutionalized, and he saw in her again the woman he had first married. He persuaded the authorities to allow her to visit him on weekends, provided he returned her to the facility in the evenings.

Her early release for good behavior was contemplated on the condition that Jack would take full responsibility for her. Jack agreed. He paid off the lease on the cottage he had reserved for her, recovered her things, and allowed her to move into his new home with him. He bought her a new Lexus for her birthday and drew on his retirement funds to build a beautiful swimming pool and hot tub at the rear of the property. They made a deal. If Abby could abstain from drinking for two years, Jack would consider becoming engaged to her and remarrying her.

In return, Abby promised that she would remain sober and never touch an alcoholic drink again as long as they remained together. She obtained work. Eventually, though, Abby could resist no longer and began secretly bringing wine home and drinking it while Jack was at work, hiding it while he was there with her. He became suspicious when he could smell it on her breath, despite her attempts to conceal it with mints and other concoctions. She had broken his trust and her promise. It was a bitter blow to Jack. He became resentful and insisted that from then onward, they would occupy separate bedrooms in his house.

It was an uneasy situation. Although Jack felt responsible, he could not rely on Abby to keep her bargain with him, and now he wanted to be free of her again. His distancing from her made her crazy and unreasonably jealous. He sought advice and was warned that she was extremely unstable and possibly dangerous to herself as much as anyone else. This proved to be the case when finally, in a drunken rage, she threatened to kill him with a kitchen knife after he returned from work. She screamed at him that if she could not have him, then no one would. Fortunately for Jack, he managed to overpower and disarm her. He then locked her in her room.

After passing the night somewhat nervously in his separate bedroom, he called the police the next morning, and she was arrested again and subjected to psychological assessment. As Jack did not press charges, she was released on condition that she moved to another location.

Jack found and paid for an apartment for her and helped her to move out of his house with the things she wanted. However, he was still never free of her or her incessant calls on his telephones. He changed his numbers, but still she tracked him down. His counselor told him that his mere presence in her life was enabling her addiction, and that as long as they were in contact with each other, she would never be able to give up alcohol.

Wanting to start fresh, Jack was able to obtain another restraining order against Abby, and he jump-started his own life again—still a single divorcé. He met other women and developed friendships with men as well, including fellow tennis players and colleagues. Nearly a year had passed when, somehow or other, preying on Jack's desire for her affection, Abby convinced him that they should get together and try again. It almost seemed as though Jack was as addicted to Abby as Abby was addicted to alcohol.

His fragile friendships with others were damaged. People shrank away, beginning to think he was incurable too. They feared Abby's disastrous influence over him. They were right. He finally invited her back to his home again after another promise from her that she would abstain from drinking permanently. In a rush of emotional release, he made their reunion complete by remarrying her.

It lasted another five months before she reverted again to her addiction, repeatedly losing the jobs she obtained and driving away his few remaining friends. He applied for and obtained a second divorce from her, but not without having to make a further generous financial settlement, which allowed her to keep her new luxury car and continue living in his house by herself. She was awarded half its value if it was ever sold.

Jack bought himself another property in yet another town, which again he remodeled at his considerable expense. By now, Jack had run the course of his endurance and assuaged his sense of guilt, and he was finally able to acknowledge this, severing the emotional ties that had existed with Abby. He resumed his single life. He eventually met an attractive woman in his new town, and they began a romantic affair.

This time there was no further interference from Abby, who had descended into another series of addictive binges, alternating with attempts at recovery through rehab, applying successfully for jobs and then losing them due to her addiction.

Jack's new romance flourished. He and his dear girlfriend, Clare, became engaged. It seemed that all would be well. Unfortunately, friction started between them, and this led to serious arguments and insults, which resulted in the engagement being broken. Clare had been single for many years. She had only been married once before, for a short time. She had no children, and her career had placed her in a position of authority. Her experience in art of compromise was limited. The combination of this and Jack's driving energy and self-assurance led to conflicts. Eventually, because they remained attracted to each other, they made up. For the first time, Clare moved into Jack's house with him, and they became engaged once more.

It lasted about two weeks. Another argument occurred, and more insults were hurled. The engagement was broken off again. Clare moved out of Jack's house and was luckily able to regain possession of her condo.

Months passed, and Clare and Jack started to meet each other again tentatively and on a purely platonic basis. They liked and valued each other, probably more than anyone else. They just couldn't live peacefully with each other. They eventually rekindled their affair, but they remained nervous about making a permanent commitment. The token engagement was reinstated for the third time, but it seemed unlikely that they would ever marry or live together permanently. The engagement was broken once again.

However, the story has a happy conclusion. The couple became engaged once more. They were married in Sedona.

This true story simply illustrates how life and love can affect or even damage people.

While some may be capable of sustaining a marital relationship, their judgment of others and their willingness to reach compromises can be impaired. When one yearns for that precious marital bond, desiring it almost more than anything else, and envying it immensely in others, it can lead one to act impulsively, superimposing one's ideal unfairly and inaccurately on the object of one's desire.

Maybe that is what falling in love amounts to—some sort of partial self-deception or even a kind of epiphany. Whatever it is, it can present difficult expectations for another person to meet.

It is somewhat akin to the choice you make when buying a car. Having chosen a make, model, year, color, and the features that seem best suited to you, you may discover after driving it for two or three months that maybe you should have picked a bigger car or one with a sunroof or with leather seats instead of fabric. Yet it is too late to take it back and too early to trade it in. So you choose to keep your car, enjoy it, and make it work for you. Not everything is going to be perfect in a marriage either. There will be obstacles to overcome, but you made your decision, and now you can choose to enjoy it and make it work. Jack and Clare have chosen to do this.

Part Two

Social Interaction

Chapter Four—Is It Ever Too Late to Date, to Mate, to Tarry, or to Marry?

Age does not protect you from love, but love, to some extent, protects you from age.

—Jeanne Moreau

The mature single person may have acquired certain baggage that can be a roadblock on the path to a new relationship. Property, belongings, status, career, and offspring can all play a part in deterring a person from totally merging with a significant other. For reasons like this, it may be an individual's preference to pursue a romantic relationship earnestly but without wishing to make a permanent commitment to it.

The burden of responsibility for another may also be a deterrent to marriage for a mature single person. Health issues can arise, possibly requiring an unpredictable degree of devotion and care giving from the healthier partner. Financial concerns and the dependence of one person upon another may also form part of the equation. Adverse attitudes may have already been formed by earlier experiences.

When Ernestine retired from her teaching career, she and three teacher colleagues, who were still working, decided to celebrate the occasion together by going on a summer cruise. One of the onboard activities that excited and interested Ernestine and her other single female colleague, Lou, was dancing. Later, during the following January, and some months into her retirement, she persuaded Lou that it would be a good idea to continue dancing somewhere. Lou agreed, and as she was still occupied as a teacher, suggested that if Ernestine could discover suitable places where they could go dancing, she would accompany her.

Three months later, Ernestine asked Lou to join her in attending a dance club she had discovered. Its monthly event was to be held on Friday the thirteenth. Lou was somewhat superstitious. She had only bad experiences of that date. She decided it might be an unlucky date to venture into the unknown. So she declined. However, Ernestine persisted in her efforts to persuade Lou, who finally and reluctantly relented. It turned out to be a more auspicious date than she could have imagined.

When they arrived at the appointed venue, parking spaces were in short supply, and in her hurry, Ernestine, who was driving, cut in front of a man in another car and took the space he was about to occupy. After they entered the building and started circulating, Lou soon recognized the man they had cheated, and she felt that they must apologize to him. His name was Chet Parker, and they approached him among a group of men who were talking together. Some were seated at a table. Bill, a charming man in his late seventies, was among those standing across the table from Lou, some twelve years his junior.

After the interruption and apology, Lou and Ernestine moved away to find a table. Whether it was a subconscious intention or not is still being debated, but Lou inadvertently left her drink behind and had to return to find it. There was something in the way their eyes met in mutual admiration that encouraged Bill to ask Lou to dance, despite the competing attention of another woman club member whose name was Eleanor. It was a mixer, when people normally switch partners at defined intervals, but Bill and Lou became oblivious to the custom. They remained dancing with each other in perfect harmony and continued to do so until the evening ended. It may have been that discovery that they were perfectly matched as dancing partners that sealed their fate. From that moment on, they were destined to be part of one another's lives.

The next morning, Bill left Lou a telephone message when she was out at her regular aerobics class, saying briefly that he had enjoyed meeting her. Then he hung up abruptly, as he was accustomed to doing. Even in that rather unusual, direct manner, there was something that Lou found attractive.

They began dating and dancing together on a regular basis, and within a couple of months, Bill had moved in with Lou. While perfect harmony may not have extended throughout their entire relationship, it certainly existed on the dance floor. Bill never had to think about where he wanted Lou to be on the floor and in his arms because she was inevitably there—exactly and instinctively where she was supposed to be. Lou felt that at last she had found a man who danced precisely as she wished to dance. It not only felt good; it looked good too.

As a couple, they became prominent figures on the dance scene, and Lou became the president of the dance club where they'd first met. Bill also enjoyed singing and frequented a local restaurant and bar where patrons who were singers could perform to live accompaniment. In fact, Bill had undergone surgery to expand his esophagus, which resulted in the removal of interfering scar tissue. This improved his singing ability and increased his enthusiasm. Lou, restrained in her youth by her strict widowed father from a preferred career on Broadway, was captivated. She soon graduated from the audience to the rank of performer. In her teaching career, following her natural inclination, she had encouraged pupils to put on stage shows at her school. It was not long before she and Bill were organizing their own cabaret, which included their talented friends.

Both Lou and Ernestine were already members of a singles club for people over the age of fifty. Bill had been single for thirty-five years, so Lou invited him to join so that they could both enjoy its many activities. After her own retirement and with more time on her hands, Lou was able to recruit a number of its female members to form a dance troop, which regularly rehearsed and later performed at local nursing homes and hospitals. Retirement became every bit as busy as their working lives, while their popularity as a couple expanded on every front.

Following a divorce, Lou's daughter had moved in to her mother's home with her before Lou met Bill. It had worked quite well for mother and daughter alone. Lou bought the groceries; her daughter cooked wonderfully; and Lou cleaned up after they ate.

However, there was friction after Bill joined the household. The new romantic relationship did not sit comfortably with Lou's daughter at all, as is often the case with adult offspring, even allowing for a period of adjustment. It came to the point where the daughter told Lou that she would have to choose between her and Bill. One of the two would have to leave. Faced with this unfair choice, in the kindest way possible, Lou said that while she would always love her daughter, she could not give up Bill. The daughter moved out.

Two years later, when socializing at the dance club, Eleanor, who had been competing earlier for Bill's attention, swiveled right around in her chair to question him about Lou: "Are you still impressed?"

What could he say? There was no doubt about it.

The years flew by in a flurry of dancing, performing, dressing up, and socializing. There seemed no need to formalize their relationship. Their respective offspring had adjusted to it, Bill's rather more readily than Lou's, and a status quo was established. They were a couple—an item—and the envy of their single contemporaries. In fact, they so enjoyed the single scene together and all the friends and activities that they didn't see any reason to change their status from that of simply being lovers.

Lou had noticed how much Bill had taken to the small Maltese dog that belonged to a good friend—and how the dog had also taken to Bill. Seven years had elapsed by the time Lou decided that she would like to buy such a dog for Bill as a surprise present on his eighty-fifth birthday. Her friend found a puppy for sale, and together they collected it.

Bill was tremendously delighted. The little puppy adored him, and he was enthralled with it. They named him Barnabus. As the dog grew closer to them both, Bill awoke one morning with certainty of mind. All earlier doubts about inequalities in their relationship and the potential health burden that he might become to Lou were dispelled. Partly in jest, he turned to Lou in bed and said that since the three of them had become a family, he thought he and Lou should get married.

Lou pretended hesitation and said she would have to have time to think about it. In reality, she was in complete and instant agreement, but she assumed that Bill would prefer a simple ceremony. Imagine how thrilled she was when she learned that he wished her to follow her heart and make it a grand occasion. As she was heard to say, "It was a great excuse for a party."

As a member of an elegant local business club, Lou was able to arrange to have both the wedding and reception there. As a surprise, the bridal group was to attend in antebellum costume, and over two hundred guests were invited. It was a truly splendid affair and a testament to the couple's great popularity.

For many years, Lou had adopted the custom of sending out a couple of hundred handmade Valentine's Day cards to her many friends. This charming tradition had actually become something of a chore for her, and she saw an opportunity to end it by making her handwritten wedding invitation the final valentine effort of this kind. After all, what excuse could a "married woman" have for sending out valentine cards? The invitation took the following form:

> Froggy went a courtin' at the age of 85.
> He asked Miss Lou
> Could she see her way to
> Being a valentine bride.
>
> Plans are in the making;
> February 23rd will be our day.
> Four p.m. at the Ashford Club,
> We'll take our vows, then say:
>
> Come, you friends and family.
> We'll raise our glasses high,
> Toasting Lou & Bill in marriage,
> For love so true is nigh.

Valentines—oh, yes, and frogs—were therefore the theme, and needless to say, the occasion was brimming with love, goodwill, and delight. The surprise costumes of the bridal group caused laughter but did not detract from the solemnity of the marriage ceremony, which was performed by a dear friend who is a retired clergyman, also recently remarried. It was not only a gratifying way to formalize their loving union, but it was also an opportunity to indulge their friends and allow them to share their joy. Where did it all begin? It began with a catalyst of common interests.

Love and desire for another may overcome all obstacles, but these can be fickle emotions that change over time, as the experienced person already knows. Sustaining a loving permanent marital relationship requires a strong underlying friendship and a degree of self-sacrificing willingness to compromise.

So who can say when it is too late to consider dating, romance, and marriage? If your heart is in it—and your health is up to it—maybe it is never too late.

Chapter Five—Meeting Mr. and Ms. Right

There is only one happiness in life, to love and be loved.

—George Sand

Some people who have become single are quite sufficient on their own and feel satisfied most of the time. They have the option of company, romantic involvement, or affection when opportunities arise, without the disruption of having to share the rest of their daily lives with another. They are prepared to choose a life alone. It does not necessarily mean that their lives are lonely, though—far from it.

The subconscious effect of a father's personality upon a daughter can sometimes continue for many years. In the case of attractive Susan Glenz, it resulted in her making a series of unsuitable romantic choices, none of which ended in either marriage or children. In fact, she had almost reached the age of fifty-five before she finally accepted a proposal of marriage for the first time in her life.

What did it take to find her Mr. Right? Susan had a busy and responsible career. She owned her own home, which she shared with her much-loved bearded collie named Scarlet. To keep in shape, she attended a regular aerobic exercise group at the wellness center of a Baptist church every Saturday, and she had made friends with Lou

Keehn, another woman in the class, who we got to know in the previous chapter.

One Saturday, Lou started to recount to her the events at a recent pool party she had attended on a hot Fourth of July afternoon. It had been at a private house owned by one of the members of a singles group to which she belonged. Lou had braved the stares and comments of her fellow members and, wearing her bathing suit, launched herself into the pool before anyone else had plucked up the courage. She had just comfortably settled into a floating inflatable armchair-lounger to bask in the sun's rays when a huge man named Bill Pearce playfully hurled himself into the water beside her with such force that Lou was capsized in the wake of the splash he made. Bill, Lou's boyfriend, was not at all impressed.

"We call him Wild Bill," Lou told Susan.

Later, Lou invited Susan to visit her singles club, which Lou had continued to enjoy for several years after her romance with Bill Holton had begun. They moved on to a local bar called The Getaway, where there was a disco and dancing. While they were there, Lou pointed Wild Bill out to Susan. He was sitting alone at a table near the back of the room.

"There's my friend Bill Pearce," said Lou. "Why don't you go over and ask him to dance?"

Overcoming her shyness, Susan did as Lou had suggested and nervously approached Bill's table. "Hey, Bill," said Susan, "would you like to come and dance with me?"

Bill did not respond at all. He seemed to be distracted or daydreaming and in a fog. Actually, he was still seeing someone else at that time, although she was not present, but Susan did not know that. Sadly, Susan lost her nerve at that point and retreated forlornly to the comfort of Lou's company. She had not expected things to go that way at all. She felt more than a little embarrassed and humiliated, and she was rather cross with Bill.

On another occasion, when Susan was out with her friends, Judy and Ernestine, who were mentioned in Lou's story, they decided to stop at the Landmark Diner. After they had settled down at a table, Susan looked around the room and immediately recognized a former and rather quirky acquaintance of hers called Frank. He happened to be sitting at another table with none other than Wild Bill, with whom he was evidently friends. However, Frank soon departed, and Bill came over to join the three ladies, the latter two of whom he already seemed to know quite well. After they had been talking for a while, Susan and Bill started to feel comfortable with each other. Someone suggested that they all move on to Johnny's Hideaway to dance. When they arrived, however, Susan recognized a man that she wished to avoid. He had previously danced with her on another occasion, and he had been quite drunk and thoroughly objectionable. So she hid behind the large frame of towering Bill Pearce until the coast was clear. She and Bill then danced together for the first time, and it felt good. There was undeniable chemistry between them.

Six months passed. By this time, Susan had joined the singles club to which Lou belonged. At one of the regular weekly club meetings, Lou called to Bill Pearce as he was passing her table. A group of the members had already decided to move on to The Getaway to dance, and Lou was hoping to persuade Bill to join them.

"Hey, Bill," she said. "Would you like to join us? We're all going to The Getaway afterward."

To her surprise Bill said, "I'll go, but only if Susan is going with us."

Once they got there, Bill and Susan danced together often for the remainder of the evening, despite the many other men who wanted to dance with Susan that night. As they were leaving The Getaway and walking to their cars in the parking lot, Bill gently and lovingly kissed Susan good night and held her close in a warm embrace. Susan gave Bill her telephone number. She invited him to a yoga class, but there was a slight misunderstanding. Bill thought she was asking him to go to a massage therapist, which intrigued him considerably.

Unfortunately Bill had to break that date with Susan because he had to go out of town on business, but he did telephone her to apologize. They made another date for the following Friday, but when the time came, Bill was stuck down in southern Georgia and could not make it.

When Susan met Lou at their regular Saturday aerobics class the next morning, Lou wanted to know how the date had gone the previous night, and Susan had to admit that she had been stood up—and not for the first time. Bill had now stood her up twice. Susan had been badly let down before in her life. She was now beginning to think that Bill was going to be just like all the others.

Bill then called her to make a Saturday date with Susan at a great nightspot called Fuzzies. She liked Bill, so she thought she would give him one more chance. It was a wonderful date. The band was fantastic, and they danced a lot and stayed late. They even bought the band's CD. Everything seemed to go well for them. Susan looked incredibly attractive. She wore great clothes, including a sexy short skirt, and had a super hairstyle. Bill was totally overwhelmed. He didn't stand a chance. They found themselves even more attracted to each other.

They ended up at Susan's house, but they didn't want to rush things. It was much too precious to them to risk spoiling it. They made a contract, deciding that they would abstain from sex for two weeks. Well, fate intervened. The contract did not even last the night. Some noise in the darkness, maybe it was a small animal on the roof, frightened Susan so much that she screamed aloud. Luckily, Bill was instantly by her side to comfort her.

They lived happily together for three years. It felt right. After a couple of years, Brad, the younger of Bill's two sons by his first marriage, came to live with them. It seemed appropriate for them to be married, but Bill had not proposed to either of his first two wives; it had been the other way around. So it was simply not in his mind to do so now, whatever his feelings were. On the other hand, Susan was determined not to ask Bill to marry her. She had never been married and would never dream of proposing.

It was Bill's sister from Columbus, Georgia, who started to put the pressure on him. She could see how compatible they were, and that they adored each other. She told Bill, "You should go right ahead and marry that girl before someone else does."

Having lost her parents, Susan is very close to her sister, Nancy, and her brother-in-law, Phil, who live in Jacksonville, Florida. Phil has a friend named Harry, who much admired Susan, having met her when she was visiting. Harry was trying to tempt her to come to Washington, D.C. He was a recruiter who said he was overwhelmed with résumés and hoped that Susan would apply for a post there to help him. However, his parting shot to her as he returned to Washington, D.C., was rather vague. He simply said, "See you in D.C. when you come."

Yet nothing definite had been arranged. It was because of this loose association between Susan and Harry, and her brother-in-law's preference for Harry, that her budding relationship with Bill was not greeted with much enthusiasm.

Bill and Susan's lives were packed with work and social events—many of which involved the singles club in which they had both become closely involved. They organized games nights and many other functions that the members enjoyed together.

Bill has a niece who became fond of Susan. Susan's friend Lou and her boyfriend, Bill Holton, both encouraged Bill Pearce to propose to Susan, whom they admired, thinking she was a nice person who would make a wonderful wife for him. As Susan walked by one day, Lou's Bill said to Bill Pearce, "Look at that girl, Bill. She's a keeper."

Bill came to the realization that he had been looking for a woman like Susan much earlier in his life, but he had never found her until now. He started trying to think of a special place where he could propose to her.

His niece came to the rescue. Her idea was to invite Susan to join her and her two children in an outing to see an exhibition at the botanical gardens. However, when the day arrived, Susan woke up feeling tired and told Bill that she was going to call his niece and cancel. Bill, who had already gone to some trouble in secretly obtaining the engagement ring, was afraid the whole arrangement would fall apart. So he made a great effort to persuade her that she would soon perk up once she was on her way. Luckily, she responded and managed to drag herself out to meet his niece as planned.

When she and Bill's niece and the children arrived at the botanical gardens at about nine thirty that morning, Susan was no longer sleepy and thoroughly enjoying their visit. She was just thinking how much she thought Bill would also love it there when he appeared miraculously, taking her completely by surprise. He was smartly dressed and carrying a beautiful bunch of roses.

He knelt down on one knee and said, "Susan, will you marry me?"

Susan was speechless and totally stunned. Finally, Bill had to speak again: "Say something."

The startled Susan, whose breath was completely taken away, did eventually manage to squeeze out her response: "Yes."

It was as perfect an occasion as it could be. All that was missing was the violin accompaniment that Bill had tried to arrange with his friend Jim, who played in a local orchestra but did not quite feel up to the task. There were many visitors to the botanical gardens that day, and Bill's proposal had acquired an immediate audience, which applauded enthusiastically. In fact, there were so many witnesses to it that Bill would have had a hard time backing out of marrying her even if he'd wanted to.

Susan immediately called her friend Lou, and the word spread quickly. Her friend Yvonne excitedly offered to host Susan's wedding at her house, where there was plenty of room inside and out.

At first, Susan was not sure if she really meant it, and she started to shop around for alternative venues. Finally, when she was visiting Yvonne one day, she was looking out from the rear windows of the house at the lawn under its canopy of surrounding trees and a pasture stretching beyond it. She tried to imagine her wedding taking place there. She asked Yvonne if she had been serious about the offer, which, of course, Yvonne had been.

So they arranged for the wedding to take place at Yvonne's house on May 1, 2005, the day before Susan's fifty-fifth birthday, when she would be married for the first time in her life.

A rehearsal dinner was planned onboard a large houseboat, which took all the guests from in and out of town on a scenic voyage of Lake Lanier. They were transported there beforehand by private party buses that were fully equipped with hi-fi, pole-dancing poles, and well-stocked bars. A great party was thrown while plying through the lake's waters, and there was a wonderful feast, followed by dancing as the sun was setting. There was fun for all aboard as guests formed teams to play a game of "Bill and Susan Trivia," with prizes awarded to the winners.

When it came to her wedding day, it was Susan's unusual choice, instead of a wedding cake, to have her favorite dessert: bread pudding and whiskey sauce. The appointed caterers would be making it from a recipe of Yvonne's. The caterer was so nervous about getting the recipe right that he overlooked the whiskey sauce. Yvonne had to make it herself at the last minute.

It turned out to be quite a group effort. A large number of Susan's friends from the singles club had spent time beforehand decorating the bridal arch and the house and garden with tulle, ribbons, bows, and balloons. They even planted flowers.

Susan wore a beautiful suit, and to satisfy tradition with "something old," she chose a particular hat from a collection of her mother's. Her sister, Nancy, then searched for netting and decorations to adorn it in colors to match her wedding suit.

It was a beautiful spring day. Two large tents connected to the rear of the house covered much of the seating area and the adjoining decks. A select number of people attended the wedding service, which was conducted by Bill's brother, David, who is a preacher.

Two hundred and twenty-five guests attended the reception. A harpist had played before the ceremony, and a live band played in the ballroom afterward, where the bridal couple led the dancing. Bill insisted on a group hug, which took place on the lawn beside the bridal arch. Bill's two sons, Ford and Brad, who were introduced as the "best people," spoke kind and amusing words. Nancy was the matron of honor. The maid of honor was Susan's dog, Scarlet, who had been properly groomed for her part. It was a happy occasion enjoyed by everyone.

Over the following four years, Bill, whose two earlier marriages had ended unhappily, has often been heard saying how much he values and adores Susan. He wonders how he could have ever lived without her.

While they were taking part as members of the bridal party at Lou Keehn and Bill Holton's wedding, dressed in flattering antebellum costumes, Bill remarked to Susan, "I wish I had known you long ago, when I could have taken you in a dress like that to my Kappa Alpha Old South Ball."

It seems that Susan has tamed Wild Bill, who has now allowed his friends to change his nickname to Mild Bill.

Bill has finally found in Susan his Ms. Right, and Susan has discovered that Bill was never like all the others at all. He is, after all, her Mr. Right.

Chapter Six—It Was All in the Stars

Love must be as much a light as it is a flame.

—Henry David Thoreau

Toni Thomas was in her fifties before she finally met the first man she was to marry. Many might ask how such an attractive woman could manage to have avoided marriage, and all it entails, for so long.

As a child, Toni had a strict and protective father who expected her to marry as soon as she was old enough. Somehow, she had the wisdom to know that getting married was not the answer to her nagging drive for freedom to be who she knew she had the potential to be. Instead, she made a respectable escape by becoming a novice in a Franciscan convent, where she furthered her education. She stayed in the convent for a short while—just long enough to get her parents to realize that she wanted more from life than to be someone's wife. She continued to put herself through college at her own expense by borrowing from the bank and working part time to repay her student loans. They were tough times, but she persevered.

She was twenty-five by the time she accepted a marriage proposal from a young dentist she'd met while they were students in college. There was a difficulty, however. Her father refused to pay for her wedding, and when she had conflicts with the dentist as to how to proceed with the wedding plans, she became uncertain as to whether she could really be happily married to him. Despite the fact that they were in love, she thought, *How can I plan a life if I can't even plan a wedding?*

She had bought her own wedding dress, and after making many of the arrangements, she felt that she needed more time and space. Finally, she came to the heartbreaking conclusion that she could not go through with it.

In the process of mourning this decision, she sought the counsel of an astrologer with whom she has remained friends ever since. The threefold prediction then was that she might never marry, but if she did so, it would be later in life; she would not have children; and one day she would become an astrologer herself. This prediction turned out to be accurate.

Meanwhile, another course was being charted. Jerry Dore was married for the first time while he was still in college. He and his wife had four daughters followed by a son. Sadly, Jerry's wife became addicted to alcohol after their son was born. Nevertheless, their marriage lasted thirty-three years before Jerry and his wife divorced. He had to raise and take care of his young family, but the day came when he realized that despite his success as a business executive, their lives as a couple were unfulfilling. Once their daughters were fully grown and their son reached the age of sixteen, he became unable to endure the loveless quality of his home life, caused by his wife's unrelenting alcoholism.

Two years passed before he met his second wife through the Catholic Church they attended. Jerry was wary of rushing into marriage again, and they lived together for three years before marrying. Even so, it was not a good match after all, but they managed to remain together for a total of nine years. During this time, they moved from Plano, near Dallas, Texas, to Atlanta, Georgia.

When Jerry decided to leave his second wife, he sought the advice of a marriage and personal counselor. It was an important decision because it finally enabled him to look at himself constructively and to rebuild his self-esteem and self-respect. He adopted a fitness program at a gym called Crunch. He didn't date, and he didn't socialize outside his successful career, for which he needed to travel extensively. Two years were spent alone just working on himself and improving his self-understanding. He learned to love himself and to be self-sufficient. He found that he no longer needed someone else to feel complete.

One day in August 2001, while he was working out at Crunch, he paused to look at a newspaper called *Creative Loafing*. A small classified advertisement caught his eye:

Combined dinner event to be hosted by Single Gourmet and Dolly's Party Book at 57th Fighter Group on the Sunday before Labor Day. Singles welcome.

He hesitantly called the reservations telephone number, saying that he had never attended a singles event before and was a little nervous. "I don't want to meet my next wife," he said.

He was assured that there would be no pressure, just a few friendly people getting together for a drink and dinner, with no more than six or seven at each table. Nevertheless, his knees felt rather weak as he approached the attractive venue, which was reminiscent of a WWII fighter station, complete with relics of old aircraft and vehicles of the period, a sandbagged entrance, and a host of interesting memorabilia.

Meanwhile, Toni had moved on from teaching to become a successful stockbroker, but she felt the pull of the prediction that she would one day become an astrologer—a subject she had been busy studying in her spare time. She thought she should try to set up as an astrologer full time. So, in 1995, she left the financial world to begin a full-time astrology practice.

At a party given by her friend Bobbie, whom Toni had known for twenty years, she met Terri Lee. Terri owned a business called Single Gourmet and introduced Toni to a man named Bruno. But there was a glitch. His real name was not Bruno, and he was still married, even though he declared that he was single. While she remained involved with him, these issues of insincerity troubled Toni, even though Bruno declared that he loved her dearly.

Although Toni was not a participating member of Terri Lee's Single Gourmet organization, she attended some of Terri's events as the astrologer for the group, and on occasion, would help Terri orchestrate some of her events.

On September 2, 2001, the Sunday before Labor Day, Terri found herself shorthanded for a big event she had planned at 57th Fighter Group. Terry telephoned Toni to ask for her help in hosting the event. Toni was pleased to assist, although she was not there for herself. Romance was the last thing on her mind since she was already involved with Bruno.

So guess who should be the second person that the trembling Jerry would meet on his arrival at 57th Fighter Group for his very first singles club event. It was none other than Toni, whose duties, apart from greeting the new arrivals, also included shepherding them from the entrance foyer to the bar and introducing them to those who had already arrived. Jerry managed to reduce his social activity, as well as calm his shaky knees, by taking a corner seat at the bar, where he was able to nurse a glass of red wine more or less indefinitely. The greeting table and Toni were right behind him. Neither went unnoticed by the other. As the evening progressed, the woman guests became aware that Jerry was a new man on the scene. Toni heard their interested remarks and started to pay more attention to Jerry's presence.

It is in Toni's nature to touch people she is talking to, even including the pupils she used to teach at school. Perhaps this comforting means of expression was passed down to her through her Italian ancestry. She believes it is instrumentally important when imparting knowledge, and as she explains, "When you have them by the heart, the mind will follow."

Unused to such gentle contact, Jerry was immediately impressed by her warmth and the magical transference of energy between them. As he continued to observe her, he became aware of her strength as well—it was almost as if she had an aura of goodness about her.

Jerry telephoned a day or so later to invite her out to dinner. However, it was to be part of a program. He produced a newspaper clipping listing the top ten restaurants in Atlanta. He wanted to start with number ten and work up to number one while dating Toni every Saturday night. As it turned out, number ten became their favorite—a restaurant called Spice.

On one of their Saturday night dinner dates, Toni mischievously decided to put Jerry to a test that many years ago she had devised as a way of selecting a suitable partner—or even deselecting those less suitable. She invited him into her home, where he treated her with a respect that she noted and appreciated. She then said she had a surprise for him and headed for her bedroom. Now many men would have jumped to a certain conclusion at this point, but Jerry waited patiently for her to return. When she did return, she was wearing, of all things, a piano accordion, which she had learned to play as a child. Instead of making lame excuses for leaving rather abruptly, as others had done before him, Jerry was delighted when she played for him. Finally, he interrupted her and asked her if he could have a go at it himself. It was then her turn to be surprised.

She discovered that he too had learned to play the instrument much earlier in life, and he owned one as well.

A romance had begun to progress from their friendship, but Toni was still involved with her boyfriend, the so-called Bruno, who was hanging in there, trying to resolve the issues between them. "Bruno" was insistent and invited her out on a day that she had already arranged to meet Jerry. With her loyalties divided, Toni finally decided to break her Saturday night date with Jerry in order to settle matters with Bruno. She feigned illness when she made her excuse to Jerry. The evening ended with an all-night discussion with Bruno in the kitchen of the house she had just bought in Duluth. Bruno's black truck had remained in her driveway.

Something was nagging in Jerry's mind, and he telephoned Toni at seven o'clock on Sunday morning, concerned and asking her how she was feeling. She thanked him and said that she was feeling better. Whereupon Jerry asked whose truck was parked in her driveway. Unbeknown to Toni, he had made the call from his car while parked in the street outside her house.

Thus caught in her deception, Toni then had no option but to come clean and explain the nature of her dilemma. It was uncomfortable for everyone. Bruno decided to leave abruptly to go back to the girl he had recently been dating. Meanwhile, Jerry sat in his car in a cold sweat—the understanding now dawning on him that he had fallen deeply in love with Toni, and that now, through spying on her, he felt he was about to lose her. He would have driven away at that moment if Toni, in her haste to deal with Bruno's departure, had not said quickly on the telephone to Jerry, "Stay where you are. Please don't go."

He was further fortified by an earlier conversation held with Toni's friend, Bobbie, who had said to him that she did not believe that Bruno was at all the right person for Toni.

When the dust had settled and Toni eventually invited Jerry into her house, they talked together nonstop for many hours. Jerry felt that even if he was not to be Toni's boyfriend in the future, it was important to him that she should be dissuaded from making the mistake of continuing with Bruno.

It became clear to Toni that Jerry had her best interests at heart, that his feelings for her were deep and honorable, and that he was prepared to give her up himself as long as she resolved the unsatisfactory position with Bruno. It was finalized over dinner. They discovered that they were in love with each other. So Jerry moved in with Toni in Duluth—to live happily ever after.

Early in this relationship, a mutual friend named Robyn Bartlett, with whom Toni had been promoting her astrology business, decided to make an example of the happy couple. Robyn was the organizer of a socially interactive group called Single Mingle. Members were asked to speculate on which dating members would last two years with the same person. Jerry and Toni were the couple that earned the most votes, and a party was held by Single Mingle in their honor. This was an important milestone for Toni, as none of her earlier relationships had lasted that long.

Four years passed in utter bliss. They were in perfect harmony. There were no arguments, just fun and pleasant surprises, with both of them wanting each other without needing the other to complete them. It was a good and wholesome balance. Toni's astrology business prospered and so did Jerry's lifelong career with the same company. Marriage was never even discussed. They were best friends as well as lovers. Toni was Jerry's "queen," and she jokingly made him her subject and her servant. Never in her life had a man taken her clothes shopping, which Jerry did habitually. He was aware of the deprivation she had suffered in her earlier life and was determined to make up for this by spoiling her as much as possible. He bought her mink coats and dresses repeatedly, giving her a bigger wardrobe than she had ever owned.

Shortly before their third Christmas together, on December 22nd, Toni's widowed father died. With this sad news, they had to leave all that had been prepared at their home, the decorated tree and all the wrapped presents beneath it, to drive north to Loraine, Ohio, to be with Toni's bereaved family. The weather was bad, and they arrived in a snowstorm. It was so cold that the funeral had to be postponed until after the holiday. Toni's brother, her only sibling, went back to his own home. Her remaining cousins also went back to their homes. So Jerry and Toni were left by themselves in the deceased father's empty house, where Toni expected to remain until the weather improved and the funeral could take place. Jerry then made an unpopular decision. He announced that they were driving back to Atlanta for Christmas, where everything awaited them at home. Although she complied, Toni was cross and refused to talk to Jerry all the way home. It was a fourteen-hour drive back to Atlanta. He had never seen her like this before. She felt she was somehow letting her family and her father down by deserting his house.

They arrived back in Atlanta early Christmas morning and went quickly to sleep. As she fell asleep in her flannel nightgown, she was still angry with Jerry for wanting to leave Ohio, thinking they wouldn't go back for her father's funeral. When she woke up a few hours later on Christmas morning, she decided to make the best of things. It was Christmas after all—the season of goodwill.

Toni knew that Jerry liked chocolate chip cookies so she began to make breakfast and cookies for Jerry. When Jerry smelled the aroma of freshly baked chocolate chip cookies pervading the house, he realized that Toni's attitude had mellowed, and he produced the Christmas gifts he had carefully wrapped for her to open. There was one special gift, almost like a Russian nesting doll, where every box she unwrapped contained yet another smaller one inside it. When she finally reached the innermost one, she found a beautiful ring that she had admired when they had visited Key West on one of many trips together, and which Jerry had secretly returned to buy for her.

No wonder he had been so desperate to hurry back to Atlanta. He placed it on the third finger of her left hand.

"What does this mean?" she asked.

"Oh. It just means we're friends. What do *you* think it means?" said Jerry.

"Does this mean we're getting married?" asked Toni.

"It rather looks that way," said Jerry.

After Christmas, they were able to return in perfect time for her father's funeral in Loraine, Ohio. Everyone was accepting, and their future together was official. They bought a larger house together in Roswell and rented out Toni's house in Duluth. Finally, they were married according to astrological calculation on the auspicious date of Sunday, September 25, 2005.

It was a beautiful evening at their friend Bobbie's lakeside house, where a catered reception among their many friends preceded the ceremony, which was held under a canopied pergola overlooking the lake. It ended with fireworks and photographs, after which the happy couple rejoined their guests at the house. Each guest received a party favor in the form of a CD of delightful love songs—the cover of which bore an attractive photo of Toni, Jerry, and their little dog, Channel. Channel—a shih tzu-poodle cross—was actually dressed as a bridesmaid.

Wedding Vows

Jerry said:

"Toni, sweetheart, I promise with all my heart and soul to continue to treat you like my queen. I know that one person cannot make another person happy. Only I can do that for myself, with the help of God.

"I can tell you this, Toni, that ever since I met you, you have made me want to be a better man. You've lifted me up, you've inspired me, you've increased my joy every single day.

"Toni, you are the most sincere, most wonderful, most honest, most giving, caring, and faithful person I have ever met. I mean that sincerely, with gratitude and awe.

"I would like to take you on this day, September twenty-fifth, two thousand five, as my wife."

Toni said:

"Wow. I do know the woman who brought us together is here tonight. She brought a gift to me. You are God's gift to me. I've always said that from the day I met you. You are very special. I love you and will love you forever. I promise."

After the vows, two evocative and moving songs were played on a portable CD player. Each had been specially chosen, one by Jerry and the other by Toni. The titles of those songs were "Nothing Will Ever Be the Same" and "If Someone Like You Loves Someone Like Me."

Their vision is to continue to grow together through mutual respect and love for each other, every minute of every day, no matter how long they are together. They intend to continue to uplift each other emotionally, spiritually, intellectually, and physically. Every day, they celebrate what they have been given to the fullest, and they strive to help others through example and support.

Chapter Seven—Taking It Easy

I have learned not to worry about love; but to honor its coming with all my heart.

—Alice Walker

After a period of living the single life, there is also the question of having to share personal space with another, as well as the actual living space. This may be much harder for the childless single person who has no recent experience of such constant sharing. After years of being accustomed to the sole use of one's space and possessions, to find the closets full of another's things, one's own space limited, the kitchen shared, and the TV no longer watched at one's own discretion, it is possible to detect sources of irritation or friction. Combined with other issues or misgivings, even this could deter a person from making a permanent commitment. It did not do so in the case of Jerry Sanders and Mary Copes Jones.

Ovarian cancer usually takes its victims sooner rather than later. Yet somehow, attractive Barbara Sanders courageously prolonged her life for a whole three years before she finally succumbed in February 2004. Her death was a bitter blow to her loving husband, Jerry, who had married her forty-nine and a half years earlier. They had been high school sweethearts.

Jerry is a consummate musician and plays both the clarinet and the saxophone in local dance bands. His home has become something of a museum of art deco sculptures and paintings of famous musicians and instruments. He is also a keen sailor and has an extensive skipper's résumé. When she was alive, Barbara used to race sailboats with Jerry, and they also used to cruise the coasts of the United States and the Bahamas in their chartered sailboat together. He also liked scuba diving. Not having any children had given them the freedom to travel and pursue their common interests more thoroughly.

Sadly bereaved, he found himself unwillingly single again at the age of seventy and hardly ready to venture into an unfamiliar social life on his own. Retired by then for several years, he had more time to enjoy playing golf. Friends on the golf course introduced him to a group of golfers who belonged to a singles club. In due course, he joined and attended social meetings of the club. He dated several women who were members. He liked their company very much. He found their friendship comforting, but he had no real intentions of remarrying.

Initially, he had thought that his advancing age was going to present an increasing impediment to marriage, and that perhaps he should start looking for a wife. However, in time, he found that he had begun to enjoy the freedom of being single. Besides, despite their good company, he had not met anyone among his female friends whom he considered a compatible partner. Now at the age of seventy-three, what did he think he was doing? He became content to allow things to remain as they were.

Jerry's popularity, calm, kind manner, and levelheaded approach eventually caused him to be elected to the board of the singles club. Meanwhile, his good reputation became a talking point among the female club members, and this made a particular impression on Mary Copes Jones. She began to realize that Jerry was an unusually nice man.

She had been a member of the club for many years and had dated a number of men who were members. Divorced from her first husband after thirty-nine years and having three adult children, each of whom had produced one grandchild, she had no inclination to get married again. She was content. However, her close friends seemed to think that she and Jerry Sanders would be a good match. She said to herself, *Well, I have already kissed all the toads. So what?*

Over the years, her name had been put forward many times for election to the board. Although she had taken the lead in coordinating a number of activities, such as hiking and bridge, she had not really wanted the extra involvement of being a board member and had consistently declined. However, she now perceived that her election could present an opportunity to work more closely with Jerry and enable her to know him better. So this time she accepted her nomination and was duly elected to the board.

In the spring of 2007, at one of the club's monthly events known as a "Lunch Bunch," she planned to sit next to Jerry. Another member, Sue, chose to sit on the other side of Jerry, and she started a conversation about music, which seemed to interest him. Sue belonged to a choral group that was going to perform at the Trinity Presbyterian Church. Sue made a point of inviting Jerry to come and hear her sing. As an afterthought, she added, "Bring Mary Copes too."

For this, Mary Copes will always be thankful to Sue. Jerry called to pick her up to attend the choral performance. Afterward, as they were in a church where certain rituals are observed, the audience was encouraged to offer a prayer together, and in the process, members were asked to hold hands with their neighbors.

When Jerry held Mary Copes's hand, it was one of those magic moments that words cannot adequately describe. Is it electricity that passes from one person to another? Is it something chemical or some irresistible charge of energy? Whatever it is, it happened between these two people at that instant. Yet, in fairness, neither could easily acknowledge the fact immediately. Perhaps if either of them had done so, the spell would have been broken, and the other person would have retreated. As it was, the matter was left tantalizingly in the air.

That was it. Jerry was not someone who would push and demand. He simply allowed the natural flow of life. It would be what it would be. This gentle and tolerant attitude suited Mary Copes well.

The next group event that offered an opportunity to share a meal together was at a Joy Club dinner, where forty to sixty friends gather once a month. This time, Mary Copes decided not to seek a place next to Jerry and simply let him choose his own seat. Instead, she joined a table where her friends Lois and Sam were sitting. Of course, she was inwardly pleased, and also somewhat relieved, when Jerry came over and casually chose the chair next to hers.

Mary Copes has slight difficulty in hearing. So when Lois made the remark that she no longer dared wear sleeveless tops, like the one that Mary Copes was wearing, Mary Copes was unable to hear her and asked her to repeat it. When she did so, and Mary Copes still did not hear her properly, Jerry leaned over to her and said, "Lois says that she has given up wearing sleeveless tops like the one you are wearing, but I don't think you need to worry about it. You look beautiful."

After Jerry had been serving on the club's board for a while, he decided that he wanted to offer to host the club's annual July Fourth party at his home. It was equipped with a large swimming pool and hot tub in a secluded setting. Uncertain whether his property was up to the required standard, he asked his friend and fellow board member Mary Copes if she would kindly come over to his house to give her opinion of its suitability. He thought she could help him assess what might need to be done to improve it. She was pleased to be consulted and assured him that once it was tidied up a little, it would be a perfect venue for the party. She told him that this group of people had even held parties in garages before this, and his anxiety was quite unfounded. Nevertheless, it still worried Jerry. So he conscientiously spent time repainting rust spots on his gates, decluttering his tables and shelves, and repapering his drawers and cabinets.

The 2007 party at his house went off without a hitch. Everyone enjoyed relaxing in and around his pool as the dappled sunlight streamed through the shady trees on a hot summer afternoon. Stalwart male members—withstanding the additional heat—grilled the traditional hamburgers and hot dogs on Jerry's outside grill. They played board and card games indoors, and they played pool in his basement. It was a great success.

One of the things that Jerry found he could do without restriction, now that he was single again, was to watch baseball on TV whenever he liked. During his marriage, it had not been something that he and Barbara could share with equal enthusiasm. He had now found in Mary Copes a fellow devotee. They particularly enjoyed watching the Braves together.

During the early fall, after some guests had finally left and the clearing up was done, Jerry and Mary Copes had the place to themselves and continued to while away the remainder of the evening in and out of the hot tub and the pool. They spent their first night together.

At Christmastime, some mutual friends who own a second home on Pine Island in Florida invited them both to drive down to stay with them. It was a long journey, so Mary Copes suggested that they might like to stop for a night at her son John's spacious home on the way.

Bill and Louise, their friends who invited them to Florida, had already discreetly checked to find out whether the couple preferred to have two bedrooms or one, and they were assured that one would be just fine. However, when it came to staying at John's house, the matter of sleeping together took on a new perspective from Jerry's point of view. John and his wife had a thirteen-year-old daughter named Hannah. Jerry, still the outsider to this family, started to feel a little uncomfortable about the example of Hannah's grandmother and her boyfriend shacking up together under the same roof. Maybe it would have helped his understanding if he had ever had children of his own. He might have rested a little easier if he had realized that Mary Copes was quite unconcerned.

Later he learned why. John and Hannah's mother had conceived the child while they were both going through medical school, but they chose not to get married. They went their separate ways after they graduated. Baby Hannah stayed with her mother, but John was a frequent visitor, and both continued to be excellent parents. It was not until thirteen years later that the parents finally decided to marry each other. Unbeknown to Jerry, Hannah had already developed a broader view through her upbringing in an open relationship. Mary Copes would not have imagined her own example having the slightest effect on Hannah. However, the fact that he was even sensitive to it did expose the considerate side of Jerry's nature.

Back at home, the couple started taking dancing classes together at the Knights of Columbus. They became closer day by day. Mary Copes admired Jerry's mind and was grateful for his good health. Compared with many, he seemed such a normal person. There was nothing strange about him.

They took a spring day trip by bus to Georgia's Little Grand Canyon near Lumpkin, which is south of Columbus. In that same spring of 2008, the singles club also arranged a weekend in North Georgia on Lake Chatuge. As board members, Mary Copes and Jerry were responsible for most of this event's organization and smooth running. At the same time, they were trying to keep their relationship as secret as they could from fellow members of the club—in case it might affect their status.

Unfortunately, Jerry became ill with bronchitis shortly after they arrived. It had a debilitating effect on him, and he became rather withdrawn and unable to join in the activities they had planned for the other members and themselves. Mary Copes mistook this change in him for a change of heart about their romance and said, "Maybe you would be better off without me."

Sitting outside on the porch of their chalet overlooking the beautiful lake, Jerry made his excuses and begged Mary Copes, "Please don't go. You're not backing out on me, are you?"

After he had returned home and recovered, he reaffirmed his love for her and his good intentions toward her and made it clear that he wanted her around. In any case, he had already concluded that there would never be another Mary Copes coming along in his lifetime. She is honest and faithful, just as he is. They are well suited.

In June 2008, Jerry was daunted by the prospect of visiting Mary Copes's family in Florida at their annual beach gathering. "No," he said, "I won't go. You can go on your own. There are more than a dozen of them, and it's much too overwhelming for me with all those tests and competitions they run there." Mary Copes couldn't have persuaded him even if she tried.

On August 1, 2008, Mary Copes moved in with Jerry. Neither had ever expected to find such a compatible partner in each other.

There came a time when Mary Copes said to Jerry, "What are we going to do? You have two choices. We can go on living together … or we can get married."

Jerry already knew that Mary Copes was all that he desired in a woman. Nevertheless, he suggested that they continue living together on a trial three-month basis. If all was well at the end of that period, they would plan a date for their wedding.

Neither of them wanted the burden of having to plan and organize a large wedding and reception with many guests. Such matters can easily snowball into something with a momentum all its own, with accompanying costs spiraling upward. So they settled on the idea of getting married in Las Vegas. It was to be something simple outside the town—not conducted at a glitzy hotel chapel or by an Elvis Presley impersonator.

It was after this that Mary Copes consulted her accountant. She wondered if there was a tax ramification that might affect their choice of a wedding date. The accountant seemed to think it would affect Jerry more than her. When she returned home to talk to Jerry about it, she said, "My accountant thinks we should delay the wedding date until after January first."

"Las Vegas will be much too cold at that time of the year," said Jerry. "If we are going to go to Vegas, let's go soon. I'm going to book flights for November."

In October, they visited Niagara Falls. They traveled into Canada and explored the Niagara River. They purchased a large wall sculpture in semirelief.

"Where are we going to hang this at home?" asked Jerry.

"A good place for it would be where that large painting hangs, that one of Barbara and you racing a sailboat," suggested Mary Copes.

"Good idea," said Jerry. "That would be the perfect spot—and it is time we removed some of those memories of Barbara. It's our home now."

"That sailboat painting doesn't bother me," said Mary Copes, "but I would like to put that large mirror I brought with me from my place on the wall where you have that portrait of you and Barbara on your twenty-fifth wedding anniversary."

"Okay. We need to take that down too," said Jerry.

The wedding took place on Thursday, November 20, 2008. They had booked a nice hotel in Las Vegas and arranged for the Little Chapel on the Corner in Henderson, Nevada, to send a car to collect them.

As the time drew closer, Mary Copes suddenly experienced cold feet. She thought to herself, *I don't need to do this. I can't go through with it.* It seemed like a panic attack. It was—and totally irrational. She became more and more nervous. While she was getting ready, she called to Jerry, "Pour me a glass of wine, please, would you, Jerry?"

As she drank her wine, she began to feel a bit calmer, but her nerves were still raw. "Could you pour me another glass, Jerry?" she asked.

After her second glass, she finally felt better. *Maybe I can do this now. It's gonna be okay.*

When the car arrived to drive them out to the chapel, they discovered that it had been brought there by the minister and his wife, who was also a minister. On the journey out to Henderson, the ministers described their family enterprise. Their daughter was their business manager, and she was awaiting their arrival in Henderson. The minister's wife said that she was worried about her daughter because she had become pregnant and was not even married. She was sad that her first grandchild would be born out of wedlock.

Mary Copes was able to comfort her with her own good experience of her granddaughter, Hannah, who was also born out of wedlock, and whose parents did not marry each other until she was thirteen. By coincidence, the minister's wife had already helped to choose the name of Hannah for her own prospective granddaughter.

The ceremony was moving. It was conducted by the woman minister, who placed much emphasis on sharing, caring, and sincerity. It was a perfect beginning for Mary Copes and Jerry.

Chapter Eight—Baggage or Blessings

To love is to receive a glimpse of heaven.

—Karen Sunde

The difficulty in merging extended families can also deter a mature single person from commitment to a permanent romantic relationship. Imagine each potential partner having several married offspring with children of their own … or even great-grandchildren on the scene. Even sharing attention and affection fairly might seem restrictive on one partner or the other in their free choice of the use of their scarce time and energy. When one potential partner has no children and the other does, the impact is even greater.

Tim and Sylvia were happily married for most of their thirty-four years together. In their early twenties, when they met and fell in love, it was as though they were soul mates. They had much in common and became best friends as well as lovers.

Their life together was an interesting journey that brought them from their respective careers in England to establish a small group of businesses on the tiny island where their wedding also took place. Their families and friends flew in from England to attend. It was an exciting adventure for newlyweds. Their business expanded quickly into three enterprises, requiring a tremendous amount of energy. Labor-intensive and undercapitalized, it trapped and enslaved them. Long, lean winters were separated by short, stressful summers. After seven years, they sold their businesses and returned to England and new occupations.

Twelve years later, they were living in Hong Kong, where Tim had accepted a challenging expatriate job offer. In another five years, they had settled in Spain, where they spent ten more sunny years together. Life was a roller-coaster ride of peaks and troughs. They moved from periods of financial challenge to relative prosperity one after another.

These upheavals of home and fortune eventually took a toll on their relationship. There were no children. Mutual feelings of inadequacy gradually caused their passion, if not their affection, to wither on the vine. They remained faithful to each other, but in their last eighteen months together, events largely outside their control resulted in the collapse of Tim's enterprise and the loss of a third of their assets. Its humiliating fallout affected Sylvia severely. She was already craving security and control over her own life. Finally, she decided to leave Tim to his own devices. She returned to England. It was not her original intention to separate from him permanently, but almost inevitably, that is what happened. She subsequently filed for divorce. The settlement terms were fair, but as he bore the total cost of his losses, he was left impoverished, defeated, and temporarily out of work. He had done his best, but his grand plans for them never came to fruition.

Eventually, he managed to wind up his business operation responsibly, and he joined an expatriate advisory company, where he was able to choose a country of residence outside Great Britain. He traveled in Germany and finally settled in Belgium. Living on his own caused his life to blossom in unexpected ways. Romantic relationships developed. One in particular occurred with a younger divorced woman with whom he fell in love. Their short time together was almost magical. Almost a year had passed when his company persuaded him to come to America in 1997, where a prospective subsidiary was going to be incorporated. With his resources dwindling in Belgium, he could not afford to ignore the opportunity. Sadly, his girlfriend, whose son still depended on her and her career, was unable to join him. It was too speculative. Tim lacked assets and had no idea whether this venture would be successful.

Apart from the sadness of their parting, his progress in America seemed quite miraculous following his arrival in Florida. Unlike any earlier experience, everything just came together with perfect precision. His social and business life exploded, and he found himself enjoying the busy single life of an apparently prosperous British immigrant. He became a member of city and country clubs, chambers of commerce, and other professional groups of various kinds. He took up sailing with a retired Canadian army officer. They became friends.

When his divorce was finalized, he obtained a visa to remain and work in the United States. Until then, he had continued to commute on business trips from Belgium every three months. He bought and sold several properties profitably. After five years in the same town, with occasional romantic associations, he began a volatile relationship with a stylish semi-retired woman close to his own age. They had fun. They belonged to the same social groups and spent a lot of time at each other's homes. Eventually, they sold their respective properties and shared a new one together, which she had already purchased as an investment. After nearly two years of breaking up and making up, they finally agreed to part. It was never going to work. He was more in lust than in love, and she was unreasonably possessive and controlling. In need of a change of scenery, Tim headed for Atlanta, Georgia, where he leased an apartment for a year and continued his business from there.

It was there that a male acquaintance introduced him to a singles club. Atlanta provided his first experience of singles clubs. He had never felt very comfortable with such a focused concept, which seemed to him to smack of desperation. However, on his first visit to one of the regular meetings, he noticed a woman who appeared to be much younger than the average age of this friendly group. Her name was Yvonne. She invited Tim to the club's Christmas party, which she was hosting at her home in early December. Before then, he met Yvonne at several other balls and events held by associated singles groups.

The Christmas party was a great success. Because he was English, it typified for him an American seasonal celebration offered in a beautifully decorated home. To him, it seemed like a set from a Christmas movie. It made him feel welcome and at home again. He learned that Yvonne had a large family; their photographs were liberally displayed throughout her house. A mutual friend invited him to lunch at Yvonne's home on Christmas Day. He was invited there again on New Year's Day for lunch, and he brought with him a contribution of roasted vegetables. Yvonne's little Maltese dog, Katie, took an immediate liking to Tim and curled up in the chair beside him and went to sleep. It was a good omen.

To return a little of her generous hospitality, he invited Yvonne to the theater in January. However, before this occurred, he had the opportunity to call and pick her up for a different event when a friend was unable to do so. They were to attend a social held by the Black Tie Club. It was there that he started to fall in love with Yvonne.

They were sitting at a table talking together. He noticed that her attractive bangs were falling across her twinkling eyes, and he gently stroked them to one side with his fingers. There occurred such a loving look in her eyes at that moment that he thought to himself, *I could really love this girl. She is very special.*

Their group moved on from this event to a favorite local piano bar. Tim danced with several of the women who were mutual friends but found Yvonne's company so magnetic that he felt increasingly drawn to her. There was something so calm, positive, happy, and pleasing about her nature. Her smile and her laughing eyes seemed to light up the whole room. There was something extraordinarily good and wholesome about her. At one point, he accidentally touched her back without realizing that his hand had slipped under her blouse. His fingers touched her satin-soft skin, and the most amazing thrill ran through his body. It was like a charge of energy. Her skin seemed to melt away like gossamer under his touch. It was so fine, so perfect. She evidently felt a similar experience, for she leaned over to him and whispered, "Wouldn't you like to come home and snuggle with me?"

However, it was not on that occasion, when she was already riding home with a friend, but on another that Tim and Yvonne kissed and cuddled in the car in her driveway until four in the morning. They were giggling and laughing like teenagers. Despite her deceptive youthful appearance, Yvonne was only three years younger than Tim was. From differing perspectives, they found that they shared a lot of the same history. They had each lived through the same changes in custom, culture, and fashion. They moved indoors and sat together on a couch.

Eventually, Yvonne said, "You can't possibly drive all the way home at this time in the morning. I am going to let you stay here with me, but you have to promise me that you won't touch me."

Those were famous last words. He kept his promise for over an hour, but it was impossible to keep it any longer. Tim and Yvonne became lovers even before their first official date. However, that date did eventually take place. They had dinner at an attractive little restaurant on the opposite side of the square from the theater. Yvonne was able to meet some of Tim's friends who had arranged to see the same show.

The twentieth anniversary of the Executive Suite Singles Club was celebrated by holding the Starlight Ball. Yvonne had helped organize the event. It was a great success. At the end of the evening, when everything had been dismantled and cleared away, many of their fellow members who'd attended that evening congratulated the couple on their choice in each other. They felt closer than ever.

Earlier in February, Tim had already met Duffie, his wife, Laura, and their two little sons, Reece and Davis. Yvonne had arranged a large family dinner at her house. Tim was quite overwhelmed by the number of family guests — six adults and four children. He also noticed a change in Yvonne from the role of his girlfriend to one of family matriarch. It was stunning.

On February 19, Tim and Yvonne attended the formal Oglethorpe Ball, held annually in February by the British American Business Group. Their dates were now beginning to accumulate.

Tim started looking for a house to buy nearer Yvonne's neighborhood so that he could reduce his long commute to see her. He made a point of bringing a dozen red roses to her whenever he called on her. She said to her elder daughter living in Texas, "I think I'm being courted."

In May of 2005, Yvonne had already agreed to host a wedding in her backyard for Susan, a close friend. One day in early March, Tim was standing outside with his arm around her, overlooking the large wooded yard from an upper deck. Yvonne explained that she was worried about the last step from the lower deck to the lawn being too high. The ground below it had been eroded. She was afraid that one of Susan's wedding guests might stumble or break an ankle.

"Do you think you could build me an extra step there?" she asked.

71

Tim looked at the area and the exposed roots of a huge tree just beyond the steps. The ground all around it appeared to be uneven. It seemed to him to be as much of a hazard as the step she had mentioned. A thought then occurred to him.

"How would you like a platform built around the trunk of that tree?" he asked. "It could connect with the steps and cover all the rough ground as well. It could be shaped like a hexagon."

"Could you really build all that?" asked Yvonne. "That would be wonderful. Why don't you talk to Lee, my son-in-law, about it? He and Brooke will be over on Saturday."

"I've never built anything like this before, but I don't suppose it could be that difficult."

Tim and Lee discussed the matter and bought some lumber and materials. After a week, Tim had completed the outer frame, leveled it, and supported it on posts secured in concrete. He discovered that the ground sloped away more steeply than it had appeared to when he was surveying the site with Yvonne from the deck above. Maybe he had undertaken more than he imagined. One side of his frame was on the ground and the other was four feet above it. Instead of only one step, several would now be needed to reach the lawn.

By prior arrangement, Yvonne had arranged to visit New York with her elder daughter and grandson. She and Tim would be apart for five days. He made up his mind to ask her to marry him on the Wednesday night before she left.

He secretly ordered a solitaire diamond engagement ring. By chance, on the previous Sunday, Yvonne was talking about a ring she had inherited earlier from her aunt. She happened to mention that her ring size was unusually small—only a four and a half. A smaller ring had to be inserted inside the heirloom before it would fit her. This fortuitous news alerted Tim.

The next day, he urgently called the jewelry store to ask them the size of the ring he had ordered, only to find that it was a standard stock size seven. This was going to be much too large.

"I must have a size four and a half," he said. "Can you do it by Wednesday?"

"Oh dear," replied the associate, "We don't carry such a small size. It would have to be a special order, and that would take at least a week."

"Maybe I'd better start looking elsewhere," Tim said.

"Wait a minute," said the associate. "As this is a solitaire, it is less likely to be damaged by downsizing it. Let me talk to our jeweler and ask him if it can be done by Wednesday. Can I call you back?"

When she called back, she said it would be ready in time. She would call again on Wednesday to confirm a time for him to pick it up.

Tim then invited Yvonne to have dinner with him on the eve of her departure. He said he would call to pick her up from her home and accompany her to the regular meeting of their singles club beforehand. Tim then made a dinner reservation for seven thirty at a local seafood restaurant named McCormick & Schmick's, where there were tables set in private, partially curtained booths at the sides of the room. Tim had thought to himself, *If this doesn't go well, at least my embarrassment will be partly hidden from view.*

The young woman taking his booking over the telephone asked him, "Is this a special occasion?"

"Why?" asked Tim.

"Well," she said, "when it's a special occasion like a birthday or a wedding anniversary, we like to print a special message at the top of the menus that you will receive."

"Oh, I see." Tim said. "That's a nice idea. I suppose you might call it a special occasion of a kind. Actually, I am intending to propose to my girlfriend over dinner."

There was a squeal of delight from the other end of the line. "Oh! How wonderful." She giggled. "I don't think we've ever had that kind of occasion here before, not while I've been working here anyway. What kind of message are we going to print on the menu?"

"Umm," Tim thought aloud, "better keep it short and simple. Suppose she says no. What about this, uh, *Happy future*. That would still apply however she answers, wouldn't it?'

"Great. We can do that." She said. "How exciting! I can't wait to tell the others here."

"Would it be okay if I were to deliver a small posy of flowers for the table just after you open?" asked Tim.

"Of course," she said. "No problem. We will take care of that for you."

Before this momentous event, Tim decided to buy a new white dress shirt, which he chose by its correct neck size. However, when he unwrapped it to dress in time to meet Yvonne, he discovered that he had forgotten to check the sleeve length. When he hurriedly put it on, he found, to his surprise, that the sleeves were four or five inches longer than his arms. Furthermore, the tail of the shirt dropped down below his knees.

It was too late to change it. So he simply had to squeeze all the excess material into his trousers and haul up the surplus in his sleeves from the armholes inside his jacket. It was not very comfortable, but it was the best he could do at the time. He remembered from his distant childhood seeing expandable metal-sprung armbands that his father had worn to prevent his shirt cuffs from showing too much below the cuffs of his suit jacket. How he wished he had a pair of them now.

When he and Yvonne arrived at the singles club meeting, they circulated happily among their friends for nearly two hours. As the clock edged toward fifteen minutes past seven Tim encouraged Yvonne to wind up her conversation so that they could make a move. She was enjoying herself and could not understand why he was in such an unusual hurry to leave.

They arrived at the restaurant on time and were shown enthusiastically by an overjoyed greeter to their reserved booth. So far, the secret was safe. Yvonne noticed and admired the flowers on the table, assuming it was the policy of the restaurant. Then she noticed the message at the head of the menu and became curious. She did not say anything, but she thought to herself, *Why would they print Happy future there?*

After they had settled in their seats opposite one another and surveyed the menus for a few minutes, Tim, inching his sleeves up surreptitiously, stood up and moved toward Yvonne's side of the table. She thought he was coming over to kiss her, as he often did.

It came as a surprise to her when, instead of stooping to kiss her, he knelt down on one knee, looked into her eyes, and said, "Yvonne, I love you very much. Will you marry me?"

She was breathless for a moment. Then she smiled and said, "Yes. You know I will."

Tim then produced a small black ring box from his jacket pocket and opened it to reveal the urgently resized solitaire engagement ring, which he gently placed on the third finger of her left hand. It fit perfectly, the single marquise-shaped stone reflecting rainbows of sparkling light. Even that sparkle, though, could not compete with the sparkle in Yvonne's eyes.

They were both overcome with a mixture of emotion and relief. They were overjoyed too, so much so that they had difficulty concentrating on making a selection from the menu. Eventually, a delicious dinner was served, which included fresh lobster that was beautifully prepared. It was a perfect beginning to a perfect evening. When the full extent of the new dress shirt was finally revealed, Yvonne nearly died laughing. Tim never wore it again.

While Yvonne was away in New York with her eldest grandson, Bryton, and her eldest daughter, Shelby, Bill Pearce and his elder son Ford come over on Sunday to help Tim with the carpentry. Bill was the friend who was going to marry Susan there on May 1, so he had an interest in wanting the job done. It was a trying day. Tim had driven down early from his apartment. He was not feeling well and running a temperature. They tried to arrange and connect the measured pieces of the framework around the tree trunk by balancing them on folding chairs borrowed from the existing deck. It was a shambles. Everything kept falling down, and the calculations didn't seem to fit the site. They argued about it, and as the sun started to fall in the sky, Bill was heard to say, "This is enough to make a preacher cuss."

On that day, Tim asked Bill if he could keep a secret. He was dying to tell someone the good news of his engagement to Yvonne, but he wanted Susan to hear it from Yvonne first. So he only told Bill on the condition that he did not tell Susan. Then Yvonne could break the news to her in person after she returned. Bill was as good as his word and somehow managed to keep the secret to himself.

A week after Yvonne's return from New York, they drove to Florida and spent a long weekend over Easter with a male friend of

Tim's who was now divorced. They needed a break, and it was good for Tim to see some of his Florida friends again and introduce them to his fiancée, Yvonne.

People have often said that the path of true love does not run smoothly. When Yvonne had reached New York and broken her exciting news of the engagement to her daughter, Shelby, it was greeted with far less enthusiasm. Shelby was alarmed. Had her mother lost her mind?

From a married daughter's perspective, it seemed preposterous that her mother, now aged sixty-five and married twice before, could possibly contemplate marrying a foreigner who was not even an American citizen, and about whom she knew relatively little. One often reads about lonely elderly widows or divorcées falling prey to the charms of unscrupulous male predators. How did anyone know that Tim was not a bigamist or a fugitive axe murderer?

Although Yvonne's younger daughter, Brooke, had already met Tim and formed a favorable impression of his intentions toward her mother, Shelby's anxiety quickly spread to her husband, Mark, and her married brother, Duffie, who was the youngest of Yvonne's children.

After this, the atmosphere became tense between Yvonne and her elder daughter, Shelby, and her son Duffie. Shelby even reduced Yvonne to tears on the phone, screaming at her, "You're crazy, crazy, crazy!"

They felt that they should have been consulted before she accepted a proposal of marriage. There was suspicion. Why was there such a rush to get married? How was it going to affect them and their children? Why couldn't this older couple simply live together if that is what they wanted. What about the memory of Joe, their dear departed stepfather?

When they were back in Atlanta, Yvonne and Tim decided to deal with the problem directly and fly down to Texas early in April so that Tim could be formally introduced to Shelby, Mark, and the three grandchildren, Bryton, Collin. and Alex. After a slightly uncomfortable beginning, it soon became clear that Tim's intentions were honorable, that he loved Yvonne, and that Shelby's concerns, though perfectly understandable, were founded on suspicion and annoyance at being bypassed. Even if she had not been consulted, she felt that she should at least have known or met her future stepfather before a proposal of marriage was even considered.

Having no children or remaining close family of his own, it had never occurred to Tim that anyone else but Yvonne would have any say in whether she should remarry or not. He had remembered asking Sylvia's stepfather if he had any objection to his marrying her when the time came. She was only twenty-one then, and it was customary at that time to consult the parents of a nubile daughter. The idea that a woman's adult children should be consulted about her future marital plans had not entered his head. It was her life, not theirs. They had their own lives to lead. He had misunderstood the closeness of the bond between them and Yvonne.

The tension was relieved considerably when the grandchildren took an instant liking to Tim. It was mutual. They had a lot of fun together. As a result, Shelby's attitude softened, although she continued to feel that she had been slighted, and she kept the pressure on Yvonne to be sure that a prenuptial agreement was signed before the wedding.

Tim's work on the amateur construction of the new hexagonal deck had come to a standstill when it became difficult to position and support the inner hexagonal frame around the tree so that it was level with the outer one.

After Yvonne and Tim returned from Texas, they had to move ahead with their wedding plans as well as complete the deck in time for Susan and Bill's wedding. In a way, the fact that an important wedding in Yvonne's family was actually going to take place, after they chose a suitable date, seemed to detract a little from her children's objections. The decision had been made. There was something big being planned that involved everybody in the family, children and adults alike. It was a matter of some excitement to the children, who would have significant parts to play in it. Decisions on what to wear would have to be made. Adults became caught up in the children's excitement and in the details. It was now a matter of how and when—not whether it was going to happen.

The deck eventually came together, if not precisely where it was intended. It took five weeks off and on. Yvonne, who was suffering acute pain from an arthritic left knee, was a tireless supporter of Tim's efforts. They would start early and continue working all day, sawing and screwing the intricate spokes of the supporting sub frame. It was grueling work for elderly amateurs. The relief at the end of a hard day was unbelievable when they could soak away their aches and pains together in the spa tub in Yvonne's spacious bathroom. They made a good team.

Neighbors who had been close friends of Yvonne's deceased husband, Joe, came to see how the work was progressing and helped Tim by lending him tools and giving advice. With further help from Brooke and her husband, Lee, the project was finished within a couple of weeks of Bill and Susan's wedding date.

During the wedding ceremony for Bill and Susan, Tim became inspired by Yvonne's beautiful yard. He said to Yvonne, "We could do this for our wedding. We already have the know-how and all the contacts. All we have to do is change the color scheme."

It seemed to have become a year for weddings. At the end of May, they visited Florida again when Michele, an English friend of Tim's, asked him to give her away during her marriage to Greg. It took place on a novel floating chapel in Clearwater Bay. They spent nearly a week in the area afterward, catching up with Tim's friends and visiting some of his former haunts.

Tim told his friend Toni Thomas of his plan to marry Yvonne. Toni was an astrologer who was planning to marry her boyfriend, Jerry, in the fall. She consulted her charts and chose an auspicious and significant date for Tim and Yvonne to marry. She chose October 22, 2005, which just happened to be a Saturday. It could not have been better.

Yvonne was born in Rosenberg, Texas. Her parents divorced while she was quite young, and she'd had an unhappy childhood. She was the first person in her family to go to college and obtain a degree. While she was at the University of Texas, she met a law student named Mac. They fell in love and married while he was still in law school. After she graduated from college, she got a job and supported Mac until he graduated. They worked hard together, building his law practice. They owned a beautiful house in Houston, where the children were growing up, and they had begun to lead an affluent lifestyle.

Nineteen years later, she received a bombshell when Mac asked her for a divorce. Her seemingly perfect marriage was ending. Because of an unhappy childhood, Yvonne had promised herself that she would never divorce nor hurt her children. She was devastated. Mac decided to remarry and chose someone who expected to move in on Yvonne's social circle. Continuing in the same area became impossibly humiliating and uncomfortable for her. So she moved to Atlanta with Brooke and Duffie. By then, Shelby was already at college, and she could not contemplate moving until after she had graduated. She stayed in Texas after all, where she had met her first husband and started a family.

Meanwhile, Yvonne became a Realtor, and eventually, in 1982, she met her second husband, Joe. When Joe was transferred to Chicago, Yvonne went with him, where she continued to work as a

Realtor. They remained there until Joe retired and then moved back to the house he already owned in Atlanta. It had been occupied in the meantime by Brooke and her husband, Lee, while they were looking for a house of their own.

In 2000, Joe was diagnosed with melanoma. At his earlier request, Yvonne had already retired from her realty profession. Joe's skin cancer had spread internally before they could catch it. Sadly, he died in March 2001. It was a heart-wrenching and pitiful time for Yvonne, watching her wonderful, supportive, towering man weaken and wither away.

They had spent nineteen secure years together. Joe had been more of a father to her children than their real one had been. He was badly missed by everyone. For almost two years afterward, she hardly left her house. Her children were supportive, and they frequently took cruises and holidays together. It seemed as though her life would be focused on her children and her seven grandchildren from now on. Her son, Duffie, and his wife and their two baby boys moved from Texas and stayed with Yvonne in her home while they were looking for a house to buy. When the time came for them to move out, it was almost as tough on Yvonne as the day she lost Joe. She became depressed and lonely.

One day a former colleague introduced her to Joan, a lively and amusing companion who was already a member of Executive Suite Singles. She insisted that Yvonne come to one of the regular weekly meetings. Yvonne became Joan's project, and she took her to other clubs as well. It was good to talk to contemporaries again. Yvonne decided she particularly liked the friendly people she had met at Executive Suite Singles, and she made up her mind to join it. She soon became good friends with many of the women members. She joined in the club's activities, offering her big empty house as a convenient venue whenever it was needed. She became popular, and life started to be worth living again. Parties like those she used to enjoy hosting with Joe were taking place in her home once again. She loved every minute.

After returning from Easter in Florida in 2005, Tim, who had been house-hunting in Altanta for several months, had seen a house for sale on the same street as Yvonne's home. He'd made an acceptable offer, and the sale closed in June. As they were already engaged and due to marry in October, Yvonne suggested that he move in with her so that he could renovate his new house without having to work around his furniture and possessions. It became a profitable and imaginative project. He spent about ten months improving the property before finally selling it.

In July, they visited the family in Texas again. Life was busy for the engaged couple. Apart from their singles club activities, a wedding to plan, and the new house to renovate, there were many family visits and sports activities to attend back in Atlanta. To Tim, there seemed to be a constant flow of family members visiting, telephoning, or requiring Yvonne's presence or opinion. Initially, he had felt that he was the intruder, but as time passed, he began to feel that the family was intruding on him. He was simply not used to so many people having a perfect right to be there. He could hardly object. They were very nice people, attractive, caring, responsible, and self-sustaining. Nevertheless, being the partner without any children of his own, he started to view the extended family as Yvonne's baggage. He started to feel as overwhelmed by the family as he felt resented by it in his new role as someone significant in Yvonne's life.

When the wedding day approached, it became clear that almost two hundred people would be attending. A number of Tim's friends were flying in from Tampa and Brussels. His best man, David, and his wife, Jane, were flying in from Spain. It was just as well that Tim had purchased the house across the street, because it was going to have to accommodate ten people from Texas on inflatable beds, including Shelby's family. Special accommodations had been made at a nearby hotel for other visiting guests. Sylvia Dymond was invited to stay at home with Tim and Yvonne. She operated a successful social club in Brussels named Rainbow, on whose committee Tim had served.

As a wedding gift, Reverend Bill Stubba, a friend who was a retired preacher, offered to perform the marriage ceremony. He also sang the Lord's Prayer. Two tents were erected in the backyard, and a red carpet ran from the steps of the hexagonal deck and down the lawn to a bridal arch, which was richly decorated in white tulle and red ribbons and bows. Red and white was the theme. It followed through from table centers to fence posts, where ribbons, bows, and balloons liberally adorned the house and grounds. The girlfriends from the singles club had once again decorated beautifully.

Yvonne's son, Duffie, gave her away, despite not feeling well. When the preacher asked, "Who presents this woman?" all seven of Yvonne's grandchildren, standing barefoot like Yvonne, the boys in tuxes and the girls in long burgundy dresses, yelled out, "We do!"

Everyone was amused. The family looked marvelous. Every member was beautifully dressed and seemed to reflect Yvonne's own good looks, whether inherited or not.

For a recent assignment for his school's English class, grandson Collin was asked to write an article on a subject that had influenced his life. This is what he wrote, recalling a time when he was six years old.

Never Too Old

It was a dim, misty day, with a sense of gloom everywhere, as we made our way to the funeral. Silence filled the car as we disconsolately sat while the car drove on. We entered the church and sat in the front pew. People around me cried their eyes out as the pastor talked of the person that had died. I had a younger sense of innocence and didn't exactly understand what was happening. The only thing I could comprehend was that I wouldn't get to see my grandpa anymore. I would ask why, but I never really got an answer I understood.

It was four years after my grandpa died when my mom told me that my grandma was getting remarried. I didn't even know how to take in the fact that my grandma was dating. It just felt so bizarre thinking of how my grandpa had passed only four years before—and that she was getting married again. My mom told me the wedding would be in two months and that my brother, sister, all our cousins, and I were to be in the wedding, walking people down the aisle and such. We planned to go to Georgia a week before the wedding. For the next two months before the wedding, I thought about how weird it was that my grandma was getting married at her age. When it was nearly time for the wedding, my brother and I had to be fitted for our tuxedos. I had never done something like that before. So it felt pretty weird having this stout, plump man taking my measurements. A few weeks later, we took the plane on a two-hour trip to Atlanta. On the plane ride, I just could not believe the fact that I was about to go to my grandma's wedding.

The wedding was to be held in my grandma's backyard, which is about the size of six classrooms combined. They had set up this white floral archway above where the priest was to marry them. The overall layout of the wedding was white and crimson. I could see the colors everywhere I turned—no matter if it was outside or inside. On the day of the wedding, there didn't seem to be as much chaos as the movies and TV shows lead you to believe. The hardest part before the wedding was getting into my tux. It's a heck of a lot more complicated than it looks. When the wedding started, my cousins and I began to walk family members and other people down the aisle. I slowly marched my aunt down the aisle, with everyone looking at us. I could feel the eyes piercing me with stares. My hands started sweating, and I began to think of all the things that could go wrong. After the children had walked all the people down the aisle, my uncle walked my grandma to the classic wedding march to be wed. As soon as the "I do's" were said, I began to realize that a person is never too old to find love a first or second time. My grandma and the groom, whom we like to call Mr. Tim, are still married and couldn't be more overjoyed.

A proper honeymoon would have to wait until another time. Instead, they enjoyed a "mini moon." Tim arranged a short and luxurious stay for them at the Biltmore Inn on the famous Biltmore estate near Ashville, North Carolina. They couldn't leave until the last of their visiting guests had departed, but it was a wonderful relief to be there on their own again at last—and in such splendid elegance.

Over the next three years, Tim grew closer to Yvonne's children and grandchildren, and became fond of them. Both children and grandchildren became accustomed to him and appeared to be fond of him, too.

He was extremely touched by a recent and magnanimous gesture by Shelby. As a delegate to a charitable convention in Atlanta, she was spending a couple of nights afterward with Yvonne and Tim. They had picked her up and taken her to a local nightspot. When Tim asked her for a dance, she told him how much she now loved him, and although she thought it was justified at the time, she now regretted her initial hostility. It was very moving. It could not have been easy for her, and he realized what a big heart she had.

As a foreigner, he now has a better knowledge of American sports due to the athletic activities of the younger grandsons, Reece and Davis. Tim's stepson, Duffie, his wife, and the two boys frequently spend time at Yvonne and Tim's home. Tim even learned to be a scuba diver in his senior years. He was certified by stepson-in-law, Lee, a diving instructor and dive shop owner. It has enabled him to go diving in Key Largo, Curacao, and Bonaire with Brooke, Lee, and their children, Maggie and Chris. Tim also keeps a sailboat on a dock at Brooke and Lee's lake house, to which they make frequent family visits. He and Yvonne also go on cruises with their Texas family—Shelby, Mark, Collin, and Alex. He regards himself as being fortunate and is proud to have acquired a ready-made family through the woman he loves. What had started out being baggage has truly turned into blessings.

Chapter Nine—Run at First Sight

True love doesn't have a happy ending:

True love doesn't have an ending.

—Anonymous

Being sociable is important in the lives of single people. In reaching out to other like-minded individuals, a person is likely to find enjoyment, companionship, and even romance.

The first visit by Lois Hoopes to a meeting of Executive Suite Singles occurred in the early 1990s. She was then working for Hilton Hotels Corporation as senior convention sales manager. A friend who believed that Lois might have a business interest in common with Sam Focer introduced her to him. At the time, he was involved in the travel business. Actually, Lois had no interest in meeting a travel agent since that business had little to do with her work with conventions. Nevertheless, as a newcomer, she felt obliged to make the effort and agreed to the introduction.

Sam, a West Point graduate, did happen to be a junior partner in a travel agency. As a favor, he had lent money to a friend who owned the agency and was looking forward to having his loan repaid and then having no more to do with it. He actually worked for Property and Casualty Insurance Group and was then steadily building his own property portfolio for his retirement by acquiring rental properties and renovating others for resale. He was totally disenchanted with the travel business and had absolutely no interest in talking to a hotel person.

The introduction was based on imaginary common ground. Apart from this, Lois discovered that her first impression of Sam was distasteful. It was a case of mutual dislike at first sight. She found him arrogant and extremely rude. That first encounter annoyed her so much that whenever she attended future events or meetings of the group, she avoided Sam at all costs. If she noticed that he was present, she made a quick exit. She wanted nothing whatsoever to do with him.

She was therefore surprised when she received a telephone call from Sam one Saturday morning in 1996. He said he was going to drive out to North Georgia to look at a property in Ballground. He asked her if she would like to accompany him. As it happened, she had an invitation to a birthday party for a friend and had a good excuse for declining. *Thank God,* she thought. *What on earth would we talk about sitting in a car together for an hour or more each way?*

Sam persisted, however. Despite her misgivings, he actually sounded pleasant on the telephone. He asked her if she would be free the following weekend. He had some tickets to the homecoming game at Georgia Tech.

Lois was out of excuses and agreed to go to the game. She then saw a completely different side of Sam. He was very charming. She found him easy to talk with and actually quite attractive. This was the beginning of their romantic relationship, which continued for two and a half years.

During this time, they enjoyed traveling together to visit Sam's family in Reno—also going to Denver, Upstate New York, Pennsylvania, and Virginia—as well as visiting Lois's daughter and family in Illinois.

In 1997, Sam invited Lois to his fortieth class reunion at West Point Military Academy. She had the opportunity to meet his fellow officers and former classmates and their wives, whom she found to be completely charming and welcoming. Following the reunion, they traveled up to Cape Cod to spend a long weekend visiting with West Point friends, touring the area and taking in a side trip to Martha's Vineyard.

Sam was also a member of a barbershop chorus comprised of a group of about thirty singers. Over the Christmas holidays in 1997, the chorus was invited to sing at two performances in London as part of the New Year's Day celebration concerts. He invited Lois to go with him. They marched in the New Year's Day parade on the embankment of the River Thames in sight of Big Ben, the iconic clock tower of the Houses of Parliament. They stayed in style at the Royal Horseguards Hotel, walked around London, saw the sights, and traveled on the Underground. They visited Windsor Castle, watched the Changing of the Guard at Buckingham Palace, and strolled in Piccadilly Circus. It was a wonderful experience to share together.

When Lois had retired from the Hilton in 1996, she was honored with a lavish retirement party at the top of the Atlanta Hilton. She was also given some rather incredible gifts. One of them was an all-expenses-paid trip to vacation at any Hilton in the United States. Since she had still not used this trip, she suggested San Francisco, and Sam agreed. He had not been to the city. They stayed in a beautiful suite on the fortieth floor of the San Francisco Hilton, overlooking the bay and the Golden Gate Bridge. Despite her terrible fear of heights, Lois booked a hot air balloon ride, which took them over the Napa Valley wine-growing countryside. They also visited the famous redwood trees at Muir Woods and traveled down the California coast to Pebble Beach Golf Club, where they had their picture taken on the famous eighteenth hole.

In her spare time, Lois is an accomplished watercolor artist who enjoys painting. She attends weekly classes at a watercolor studio in Roswell. Somewhere along the occasionally bumpy road of their love affair, Sam began to notice that Lois was painting less and less. Sam admired her ability very much. His favorite aunt was also a painter and a sculptor. It was important to him to allow Lois more time to follow her talent and to move on with his own life. So he decided to break up with her. No one could understand why. They seemed so well suited.

Several years elapsed. Then one day Lois called Sam and said, "I have a gift for you."

Sam had moved into a new house. The kitchen had red wallpaper. It was the suggestion of a friend who was an interior decorator. They were both surprised that it worked. Lois brought a painting she'd made to Sam's new home. Almost as though he had saved it specially, Sam had a wonderful place to hang it. The red wall was a perfect background for the painting. He was touched and appreciative.

Several months had passed when Sam called Lois to ask if they could resume their relationship. He wanted her, and he had missed her. She had missed him as well. They were both happy to make up after so many years.

In the meantime, Lois had been asked many times to come to work for Ambassador Services Group, servicing the convention industry. When she was employed by Hilton, the principals of the company had been clients of hers. She finally decided to accept their offer. Now that they were back together again, it enabled Sam to join her on many trips to various other cities. They traveled to Las Vegas, Dallas, San Antonio, Miami, Chicago, Denver, Philadelphia, and many other places. Sam was adventurous and enjoyed exploring new places. So while Lois was working, he became a tourist and returned with an interesting itinerary of things for them to do when she was free. He would find places to see and restaurants at which to eat, also discovering what the city had to offer by way of jazz clubs they could enjoy.

Since they reunited, they have stayed together for five good years. They find themselves to be extremely compatible. They both have wicked senses of humor, which helps counter the problem of them both being hardheaded. They support each other in their business ventures, family activities, and outside interests.

They have enjoyed wonderful times traveling abroad to Greece, Italy, and Costa Rica. They cruised with friends from their singles club to the Panama Canal. When they are at home, they enjoy their membership of the High Museum and Sam's partial season tickets to the Braves games.

They continue to maintain separate homes, enjoying their personal space as well as their time together. Besides, they both have accumulated so much meaningful stuff that they would have to buy a mansion to house it all. They have found a durable balance of companionship and affection, and they look forward to many more adventures in the years to come.

Chapter Ten—Singles Club Opportunity Knocks

A heart that loves is always young.

—Greek Proverb

Sadly, in the year 2000, Nell died after forty-two years of marriage to Bob. He was left on his own, a widower, bereaved and seventy-two years old. Bob was in good health, alert, well organized and financially secure. He was also physically fit and enjoyed playing tennis regularly. After more than a year of living alone, time began to drag for Bob. He missed the love, the sharing, and the female companionship of his marriage. His home was east of Atlanta, in the small town of Lilburn, Georgia. There was not a lot going on there. Was this as good as it was going to get in what seemed to be the twilight of Bob's life?

He began to think it would be nice to meet an attractive like-minded woman—but how? One day he was attending a seniors group at the Bethesda Center. A friend mentioned that there was a dance coming up on a particular Saturday night, nearer the city, at the Dorothy Benson Center in Sandy Springs. Bob had already heard that it was popular because of its active program for seniors, including regular dances frequented by refined single women. He decided to make an effort to attend.

That Saturday, Bob dressed up in a smart jacket and tie and drove over to Sandy Springs in good time. When he entered the elegant Dorothy Benson Center, he found that he was much too early. There were two long tables set up inside, and two women in attendance—ready to register people as they arrived. Nobody had come yet.

"Are you a member?" said the first lady.

"No," said Bob. "I didn't know you had to be a member. What kind of dance is this?"

"This is a private party," she said. "It's being held by Serendipity. It's an exclusive singles club. You have to be a member to come to its events."

"Can I join it now, then?" asked Bob.

"No, I'm sorry," she said. "You have to be recommended in advance by one of the members. Your application then has to be approved at a meeting of the membership committee."

"Well, I have driven some distance to attend this dance at a friend's suggestion," said Bob. Then, looking toward the second woman, he asked her, "Are you a member?"

"Yes," she said.

"I realize you don't know me, but couldn't you recommend me, please?" begged Bob.

"It's always good to have extra men at these dances," she said, "but I'm afraid Serendipity would kick me out if I broke the rules and bypassed the committee. Look, you seem a respectable guy. Why don't you give me your name and contact details, go off and have a coffee somewhere, and come back later on? In the meantime,

I'll see what I can do when some of the board members arrive. In any case, I think I'll take a chance on you. Wait a while before you come back. Then just walk in as though you belong. I don't suppose anyone is going to stop you."

So Bob departed and crossed the street. He sat down in a McDonalds, where he nursed a cup of coffee for nearly an hour. When he returned, he did as he had been told and walked straight in as though he belonged. She had been right. Nobody stopped or questioned him.

There was only one thing that she had failed to mention. It immediately made him rather conspicuous. This event was a "po'boy" dance, where everyone was in costume, dressed as hobos and tramps. There was Bob, neatly overdressed in his jacket and tie, while everybody else was wearing ragged clothes and straw hats.

Undaunted and determined, he joined a friendly group and started dancing with various partners. One woman questioned him thoroughly, but he managed to respond with convincing answers.

It was when he was crossing the large dance floor during an interval that he noticed an attractive woman heading briskly across his path from a different direction. As their paths intersected, he paused, greeted her, and asked her if she would like to dance with him when she returned. She told him her name was Judy, and she agreed.

They danced together happily for the remainder of the evening. Telephone numbers were exchanged before they said good-bye. Even before Judy had reached her home, Bob telephoned her on her cell phone to say how much he had enjoyed her company.

The following Wednesday, Judy invited Bob to join her and several other women who were going to dance at a neighborhood bar called The Getaway. While they were there having fun, they discussed another future event. It was a ball to be held by a singles club known as The Black Tie Club.

"Do you have a tux, Bob?" asked Judy.

"I have two," answered Bob.

It was settled. From that time onward, Bob and Judy continued to expand their social life and revel in their new romance. Judy already belonged to several singles clubs. They took dancing lessons together from an instructor named Barbara Head.

Between Executive Suite Singles, Who's Who, After Hours Dance Club, The Black Tie Club, Serendipity, and others, Bob and Judy had a full social calendar crowded with activities and a lot of new good friends and contemporaries. They also had time to spend together, either at Judy's home or at Bob's home in Lilburn on the Yellow River.

Judy had already been married twice. She had six children by her first husband, a local business owner. Judy was unhappy with him and had wanted to end her marriage for many years, but she was scared. She did not have any work experience except in helping with the accounts in her husband's business. She lacked the confidence to break away, not knowing whether she could find employment that would help her accommodate and support her family separately.

There came a time, after more than twenty-five years, when she could not tolerate her marriage any longer. Two of her children were insistent that she leave and file for divorce. The decision was precipitated when her mother had a heart attack and had to be moved into a hospital. That weekend, she and three of her children who were under eighteen were able to get away. They squeezed into her mother's temporarily vacated two-bedroom apartment. On their way back through Covington to pick up some of the belongings they had left behind, Judy's daughter remembered the name of a lawyer there and insisted that Judy drop into his office.

It was a good move. Until then, Judy had had very little idea about her rights. The lawyer was extremely helpful. He assured her that she was entitled to money, child support, and help with schooling. This boosted her confidence considerably.

When Judy visited her mother in the hospital, she said, "I have something I have to tell you."

"You're getting a divorce," said her mother knowingly.

"Yes," said Judy.

It was difficult finding accommodations because most rentals did not permit pets or as many as four children. Finally, Judy managed to get a job. It was after this that she was able to find a large condo for rent in Clarkston, where she would be allowed to move in with the four children who were still living at home.

Within the Catholic Church, she joined an organization known as SWORD: single, widowed, or divorced. It was in 1983 that she met Joe, a nice man who was widowed when his wife died of breast cancer. Judy and Joe were soon married, but shortly afterward, Joe also became ill with cancer. He survived for only another nine years, sadly leaving Judy alone again.

Judy is also now a cancer survivor, but her zest for life is as buoyant and bubbly as ever. Perhaps the love between Judy and Bob could be a powerful antidote. Neither has been free of health issues, but each has been there to take good care of the other. As Judy's daughter Kathy was recently heard saying, "They are just like two little lovebirds."

When they were busy dating, dancing, and socializing, Bob said to Judy that he loved visiting her as much as having her visit him. Yet there was so much more room for her and her visiting family members in his home. So why didn't she simply move in with him?

Judy was a little taken aback. She was in love with Bob, but she thought it would be immoral and a bad example to her children if she were to agree. So they continued to visit each other's homes.

Then one day Bob's daughter, Mary, a Realtor, asked Bob if she could show him a large new house that had been constructed near the Mall of Georgia at a subdivision called Hidden Falls. Bob was impressed. The house that he viewed was sold to someone else, but it gave him an idea.

When a cruise they had planned was canceled because the ship had been impounded, another cruise was arranged to replace it. Judy signed up for it, but Bob had other plans that conflicted with it. He realized how much he cared for Judy when he started imagining the other guys on the cruise rushing to dance with her and keep her company. He was feeling rather jealous. Their friends at the singles clubs kept telling him what a good choice he had made in dating Judy. Bob quickly made up his mind and asked Judy to marry him. She accepted.

They planned to buy a house similar to the one he had already seen with Mary at Hidden Falls. In the meantime, they decided to live in Bob's existing house on the Yellow River until the new one was ready.

On September 6, 2003, Bob and Judy were married. The wedding and reception were held at Bob's house. The guests included thirty members of their families plus their friends. Bob was particularly delighted by his son's speech, which was so touching and spoken so eloquently that hardly anyone dared to follow it. They continued to live by the Yellow River until their new house was finished. They now live comfortably at Hidden Falls with a new member of their family, a little shih tzu dog named Katie.

Judy and Bob have sixteen grandchildren between them. Bob has two children—a son and a daughter. His married daughter has three children, and his single son has adopted one son and fostered another. The offspring from Judy's six children total another eleven grandchildren. Not many live close to them, but all of them stay in touch.

When Bob reached the age of eighty in 2008, he was asked to reveal the secret of his youthful appearance and physical fitness. He said, "It's a combination of regular exercise and good loving."

If Bob had not attended the Bethesda Center how would he have discovered singles clubs? How would anyone? Here are some suggestions.

- **Check the local newspapers.**

- **Visit local senior centers.**

- **Ask people.**

- **Search for singles websites.**

- **Search for singles sports clubs.**

It is sometimes better not to have to rely on the old environment but to branch out on a different path. It takes a little courage to make this kind of shift. It is a matter of taking up new activities, sports, hobbies, and entertainment as well as joining common interest groups where one can meet like-minded people who may also share similar experiences.

For example, alternative groups of people can be encountered through high school and college reunions, churches, bereavement groups, senior centers, social clubs, singles groups, gyms, sports clubs, pet-training or pet-owner clubs, and new neighborhoods for people fifty-five and over. These form only a sample of a wider variety of options. As with most steps in life, taking that first step is usually the hardest.

Part Three

The Internet

Chapter Eleven—Internet Dating

The good life is inspired by love and guided by knowledge.

—Bertrand Russell

When AARP starts sending you offers to join their organization, you realize that from the age of fifty onward, many regard you as a senior. In fact, you are not officially classified as a senior citizen until the age of sixty-five. Reaching either landmark can be quite a daunting event for those who still feel youthful. After all, age is just a number, not a state of mind.

There is a common suggestion going around that you are now over the hill, and that from this point on, it is going to be downhill all the way. Yet millions of baby boomers out there disprove this theory. They are culturally motivated, politically aware and up to date with modern trends. They are stronger and smarter. They are as physically active as ever. Being a senior citizen doesn't have to mean whiling away the hours in a rocking chair on the front porch, watching your flowers grow, thinking of the good old days. In reality, the good old days are often just beginning. With more disposable income, new knowledge and opportunities are ready to be embraced and enjoyed by everyone over fifty.

Divorce and bereavement can leave many people single again at this time of life. For some, it can be a relief. For others it creates an unbearable void of loneliness. There was a time when senior dating was a rarity. People left on their own for one reason or another were expected to live out the rest of their days by themselves. Times have changed. These days, remaining single is even supposed to increase health risks. It is claimed that studies of men discovered the following effects of remaining divorced or widowed:

- **A higher likelihood of heart or lung disease and cancer**

- **A higher risk of high blood pressure, diabetes, and stroke**

- **More difficulties with mobility, such as walking and climbing stairs**

It is probable that women face similar risks. So it seems sensible to get back out on the social scene. No longer need you rely on introductions from friends and family members. There are many who are looking for the same opportunities for social interaction. Why should you be expected to be alone when you still have so much life left to live? This is a time to have fun, make new memories, make new friends, and have new experiences. Where does one start?

There was a time when the only places to meet people were at church, in the grocery store, and at the invitations of family and friends. Now we have the Internet. This new information highway can be a gateway to a new and exciting life.

It is unfortunate that online dating has acquired the stereotype of being the last resort for the desperate. It is actually an effective place for singles to meet interesting people with much in common. Many lead busy lives and lack the time for new social activities. Others simply wish to expand their horizons and rejuvenate their social circle.

Meeting new people can be challenging at any age, but it can be especially so for a senior. After spending years alone or with one person, it is hard to know where to begin. A search will show that there are many websites dedicated to senior dating. If you are a newcomer to using the Internet, it can be a little scary at first, but there is no need to know it all to make a start. You only have to know how to log on. Hopefully, this chapter will provide some useful guidelines to dating online.

The advantage of this process is that you always have complete control, and you can exercise this from the comfort of your own home. Many people embarking on this journey hope that love will come their way through one website or another, but once the interaction begins, there appears a wide variety of opportunities to make friends and meet diverse and unique companions.

Some dating sites are free, and others require you to pay a monthly fee. Nearly all of them will allow a free trial period so that you can find out whether you like it and what it offers. Once an individual has signed on, a user profile has to be created. This involves completing an electronic questionnaire that determines such things as your geographic location, the range within which you would like your meetings to occur, your favorite foods and sexual orientation. You will also be asked what type of person you wish to meet, the qualities desired in the person, and his or her location. Your own personal profile will include a photograph of you and specific details, experiences, memories, dreams, and future goals.

This analytical approach enables users to search for their most compatible matches long before considering a meeting with anyone. Profiles are stored and retrieved electronically. They are instantly accessible and contain much more detailed information than a photo can convey. Decisions are therefore rarely based on physical appearance alone but more on ideas, background, and an overall impression of the combined presentation. Internet dating is very different from its alternatives, allowing individuals more time to deliberate before communicating with each other.

Having joined a senior dating website, you will be invited to participate in chat groups without disclosing your e-mail address, enabling you to search for other members meeting your criteria, common interests, hobbies, and pastimes. You can continue to carry on dialogues by e-mail without any need to meet in person until you decide it is appropriate. It is entirely in your hands. The fear of rejection associated with the normal prospect of dating is far less intense in an online situation, which makes it an attractive alternative means of meeting others. It has greater appeal for busy people and those with dependents and other kinds of commitments that restrict their freedom to lead extensive social lives.

Match.com considers itself the most popular dating website. It was started in 1995 as a public company. It registers sixty thousand new people every day and has posted fifteen million profiles. It has about one million paying subscribers from 246 countries. There are now many similar online dating websites catering to all types of people and lifestyles, making an excellent medium for finding someone with common interests. Of course, it covers the entire adult age range. Many believe that mainly younger people use it, but this is simply not true. It has enormous appeal to the older generation, whose members can inexpensively approach a wide variety of potential friends and companions securely from the comfort of their homes. Not since high school would a senior person have come across such a large pool of potential dates. It can quickly bring together vibrant, energetic, and enthusiastic people who have remained young at heart and seek like-minded company. This is welcome news.

Dating sites provide varied services. Some offer single women the opportunity of meeting single men. Some filter according to race, religion, sexuality, and gender.

It is sensible to form a specific objective. If you simply want to have fun and form casual friendships, then stay away from matchmaking sites.

It is relatively inexpensive. There are many free sites, but you may get more rewarding results by subscribing to a site where you are more likely to meet a partner of quality. Even if you pay twenty-five to fifty dollars to join, it is still a lot cheaper than a senior cruise, and you don't have to leave home.

There are some shortcomings to dating online. Some sites allow people to post profiles and respond to each other without charging them. Unfortunately, free sites can often attract a percentage of perverts and weirdoes. So it is wise to check them out carefully before joining. There are also people who lie about themselves in their profiles in an attempt to obtain more responses. Caution is needed. If someone sounds too good to be true, the person probably is.

If you prefer to encounter someone nearer your own age group, you may have better success in joining a specific senior dating site instead of a general service one. Some suggestions of this kind are listed below:

> www.seniorfriendfinder.com
> www.50plus.com
> www.overfifties.com
> www.seniormatch.com
> www.silversingles.com
> www.seniorpeoplemeet.com
> www.christiansingleseniors.com

However, if you prefer to broaden your spectrum, then search the Internet with Google. Some of the most popular regular dating websites are listed as follows:

www.match.com
www.eharmony.com
www.perfectmatch.com
www.americansingles.com
www.jdate.com

People you already know may refer you to others with whom they may be familiar. You may wish to join more than one service if it is affordable. You can thereby maximize your opportunities. There are many sites from which to choose. It is worth examining fee structures to discover the frequency of subscriptions.

At almost all sites, a short questionnaire will require your completion, and you will need to upload a personal photo. The photo should be recent—not an old high school one, for example. It is important to be honest when answering questions. After all, you would expect the same from the people you wish to meet. However, it is not necessary to give away too much personal information initially. Never give out your address, telephone number, or place of work. It is safer to be vague about such matters at first. Do not give out your e-mail until you know you can trust your correspondent. Instead, use a site or service that does not require it. A nickname for yourself is also suggested for your online communications, but this should say something about you that is not too provocative, titillating, or racy. For instance, golfisforme, scrappinlady, or nascargram would be proper examples, while redhotmama, ilovesex, or hotgrandma might attract the wrong types of people.

Despite what has been said about the relative unimportance of photos in the decision-making process, it is also a fact that profiles that lack a photo can receive as little as 10 percent of the responses of those that do contain one. It is therefore well worth the time it takes to provide a photo that is a good likeness. If you or your friends do not own a digital camera, webcam, or scanner, you can take a few photos and a diskette to your local Office Depot, Staples, or office supply store, where they can be scanned and copied to diskette, enabling you to add one or more to your profile. Your photo should not exaggerate or glamorize your appearance unrealistically. People will want to see you as you would naturally appear. Remember to smile and look clean, tidy, and relaxed—preferably seated and in good lighting.

When writing your description in the profile, it is better to adopt a casual but informative style, as though you were having a conversation with the reader. Mention the things you like doing in life and your objectives. By using your imagination, you can stand out from the crowd by choosing an enticing metaphor—for instance, "Mature gentleman ripe for picking" rather than "Decrepit old man wants to get hitched." It is wise for women to beware of men looking for a "nurse with a purse."

You may need to add to your profile from time to time. As you are introduced to new areas of interest, you might want to mention recent movies and books you have seen and read. You can also add new photos if you think they improve an aspect of your profile. Your description can also include the qualities you are seeking in a potential partner.

It is probably a good idea to prepare the text of your description in a word processing program on your PC, where you can play around with the content at your leisure while you are off-line. When you are quite satisfied with the final version, you can then simply cut and paste it into the space allotted for it on the website.

Many sites, such as yahoo.com or hotmail.com provide free e-mail accounts. You may wish to set up an alternate e-mail address of your own so that your primary one is not exposed to the possibility of spamming.

Once your profile is online, you will want to check the site frequently—maybe several times a day. Those who have been browsing it and have seen your profile may communicate with you, and you might wish to respond—but only if you choose. This is usually done through the website's system rather than by e-mail, but in the course of several online discussions, e-mail addresses might be exchanged. It is up to you. You are not obligated to give anyone your e-mail address, and you may choose not do so until you feel that the recipient can be trusted. You can browse other profiles as much as you like. Be as positive and proactive as you can. If anyone interests you or catches your eye, you can send the person an instant message.

You can control the pace of communication. There is no need to rush things. Take all the time you need. Keep up a correspondence until you and the person you have selected feel comfortable with each other. This is a big advantage over other means of meeting people. Before you ever find yourself face-to-face with anyone, each person has a clear idea about the other. There is no need to limit the number of people with whom you are in contact through the site. The wider your coverage, the better your chances are of finding a good match. Play the field and have fun.

Initially, however, it is advisable to proceed with caution. Avoid giving out too much information of a personal nature that could be used against you—particularly concerning your finances. This includes things like your bank account number, PIN number, credit card details, and so forth. If the person with whom you are in contact presses you about such matters, then break off all communications with that individual. Keep your eyes open for any signs of fraud, cheating, or obscenity. Try not to be swept off your feet by sweet nothings and good looks. Make sure people are consistent and can keep their stories straight.

Look for sincerity and willingness on the other person's part to respond to your remarks as well as inform you. What you see is not always what you get. Photos can be manipulated. Words can lie. People may not live up to the lifestyle portrayed in their profiles. In reality, some may not resemble the photo posted on the website at all. So be prepared for both the best and the worst. If you encounter dishonesty, then end contact immediately. It is no way to start a relationship.

As far as you are concerned, try to treat others as you would wish them to treat you. Be positive, natural, and sincere—and always be polite. Return calls and answer messages, even if it is just to say that you can't talk right now. There is no need to restrict all your communications to written messages. When you feel the time is right, call by telephone. Much more can be learned about each other through hearing the way people sound when they speak, not just what they say in their online chats. However, it is wise not to use your home phone initially. A cell phone would be preferable. Be careful before your first meeting.

There are many reasons that one should take precautions when embarking on the online dating scene. Scammers abound in life. They can appear extremely charming and friendly. They submit false profiles full of lies that hide the facts and present you with illusions that may not be revealed until you have wasted your precious time stripping away the veils. The Internet is an open book, and too much personal information can enable unscrupulous men and women to obtain your home address and turn up on your doorstep, endangering you and your family. Always use the e-mail facility provided by the website or use an anonymous e-mail account. For the same reason, never use an e-mail address associated with your place of work. Spammers use online dating services to flood people with junk mail. So never reveal contact information just because it was requested sweetly.

Stalkers, rapists, and murderers can easily use the anonymity provided by online sites to find their next victims. So follow your gut instincts and apply the safety rules. Online dating sites are even used by convicts and drug dealers. Even though security measures are in place, it is impossible to verify everything. Take your time and don't be in too much of a hurry. Married people may use online dating facilities as a means of cheating on their spouses. Unless you are comfortable being the "bit on the side," it is recommended that you try to avoid such encounters by talking extensively beforehand. A sense of the situation confronting you will inevitably be revealed.

There are many advantages to online dating, and these words of caution are not intended to deter you—only to guide you. Thousands of men and women have dated successfully using online sites. So please don't be scared away by these obvious dangers. The main advantages of online dating are as follows:

- **Safety**

- **Security**

- **Affordability**

- **Openness**

- **Low risk of rejection**

- **Avoidance of undesirables**

- **Fun**

How do you spot a liar? How would you know that the person you are about to meet is not deceiving you? Trust your instincts. If red flags appear during your online chats, it may be an indication to end it and move on. Most people understand the need for caution, and any worthy correspondent will understand when you are trying to protect yourself. Plenty of online services can provide background checks, for a fee, which you can apply whenever necessary. Again, this is something that should be acceptable to anyone under your consideration. Everyone is in the same boat. Not all people online are necessarily good people, but neither are they all bad. They are just people. Be careful of those who want to rush you to face-to-face meetings and pressure you for personal contact details when they are not willing to give you theirs. Look out for inconsistencies and conflicting information between conversations. This can often be a warning to you. You will quickly learn to separate the genuine from the fake.

You may wonder how flirting goes down online. It has always been part of dating, after all. Yet flirting online is a little different. It requires a slight shift in style toward messages that are upbeat, short, and lighthearted yet sweet and simple too. Any questions should be easy to answer. Humor is the greatest tool in online flirting, as long as it is in good taste. Deliver your messages with confidence and use honest compliments whenever they seem to be appropriate. Try to ignite a spark. Make it sound cute without sounding predatory. Have fun inventing your own form of pickup line. There is no need to overdo it. Be careful not to be too suggestive and avoid making too many sexual remarks. The situation may develop into something for which you were not prepared.

Imagine now that you have engaged for some time in a dialogue with someone who interests you. The next step is to meet face-to-face. What is the best way to go about that first meeting? By now, you have become comfortable with the person you want to date. It feels right, and there is trust between you. You might be tempted to rush right out to a meeting. However, you only know this person from what you have been told and what you have seen from the photo in the profile. Everything you know may be perfectly true, but even so, some caution should still be exercised when approaching the first meeting.

It is important to arrange the meeting in a public place during daylight hours. You don't really want to meet a relative stranger on a dark night where there is no one else around. Have your own transportation. Don't arrange to be picked up from your home. Make sure you have plenty of fuel in case you want to make a quick departure.

It would make sense to meet for a coffee in a local café. Museums or art galleries would be good alternatives as long as there are going to be plenty of other people about. You might even arrange to meet among friends to relieve any tension and diversify the conversation. Tell someone else where you are going and make sure a friend or family member knows the time and place. This could also form part of your exit strategy, which is a good ingredient in your plan. Carry a cell phone with you if possible. You will want to be able to communicate with someone if things go wrong.

Avoid being committed to meeting at your home. There is a certain comfort level in familiar surroundings, but if things do not go well, you cannot leave easily, and it might be hard to get rid of your date without resorting to force. For similar reasons, it is also inadvisable to meet at your date's home. It is better to stick to public places and neutral ground. Be completely sure that you truly want this first face-to-face meeting and do not bow to pressure for it if you are not quite ready. It is not a race.

When you are on the first date, steer the conversation away from personal details. Keep it general but try to include specific things about your life that will round out the other person's knowledge of you. Watch for any displays of violence or sudden outbursts that might indicate emotional problems you are not ready to handle. Be aware of any attempts to control you. Split the bill if you are meeting at a restaurant. Neither party should be under obligation to the other. Avoid alcohol if possible, but if you are drinking, always keep your drink in sight and don't drink too much. Relax and enjoy yourself but stay alert. Let your conscience be your guide.

The purpose of the first date is to find out whether there is going to be a second date. Therefore, it does not have to be a long one, and if it is not meant to go any further, little time will have been wasted, and any discomfort will have been short-lived. You may have been out of the dating scene for a long time, and it may be daunting to return to it. Seniors are not alone in this. Just relax and be yourself. The first date is the most nerve-racking aspect of dating at any age. It is exciting, but the questions of where to meet, what to wear, how to behave, and what to talk about can seem insurmountable. You wonder whether you will like each other … and how much.

Before you meet each other for the first time, try to think of activities that you can both enjoy together in the future. Consider attending a play or a concert, arranging a picnic, visiting an art gallery, or playing golf, tennis, or some other sport together. You might even plan to spend an afternoon at a winery, browsing books, or simply having coffee together. Movie matinees combined with a meal before or after might work too, but remember that a first date should provide opportunity for conversation so that you get to know and understand each other. Managing it that way may lead to a second date.

It is a good idea to have a backup plan in case the first one doesn't work out. This is particularly important if you plan to meet outside somewhere, like a music festival or a county fair, and inclement weather intrudes. You might plan to meet at a restaurant nearby instead. In any event, the first date should not go on too long. A couple of hours are normally sufficient. It can always be extended if it is going well, but you don't want to be stuck in an all-day event if you realize after five minutes that the other person is not right for you.

Be specific about the dress code for the chosen venue. It can lead to embarrassment if one person is correctly attired and the other is not. Be complimentary to your date but try not to overdo it. Find that one thing you admire and comment on it. It can make a person feel special—but persistent comments can become irritating. Try to listen as well as talk. Find a balance so that neither person dominates the conversation. Avoid comparing your date with a former partner. Everyone has his or her own endearing qualities that are unique. Concentrate on those. Regain the charm you had when you dated when you were young, but be sincere and honest too. It is okay to kiss on the first date these days, but sex is not normally appropriate. In order to stand out, men should end the date politely while making sure they have shown that they are interested.

If the date went well, it would be a good idea to send a message afterward, saying thanks or that you had a great time. If it didn't go well, there is little point in continuing the dialogue, as this might be interpreted as stringing the other person along unnecessarily.

It is recommended that women avoid wearing clothing that is too provocative or sexy on the first date. This will create a lasting first impression that could be a misleading one. The wearer should try to dress in a manner that instills confidence while being comfortable too. Tight or uncomfortable garments and ties can spoil the enjoyment of an experience that is likely to be somewhat tense in any case. The purpose is to get to know each other, so distractions should be limited as much as possible so that each person can concentrate on the conversation. This can include questions about life, hobbies, work, and sports. Keep things light and upbeat. Try not to wear too much perfume or cologne. If the scent is too strong, it can be distracting. However, it is important to brush one's teeth and use a mouthwash or bring some mints if you are eating out. Above all, have fun. It may seem a little intimidating returning to the dating scene again, but it can also be rewarding, if only for its varied companionship.

Everyone has to know how to survive a bad date occasionally. There is no excuse for a person who behaves rudely or obnoxiously on a date. It is better to walk away from it. If you are the one who is too nervous, then cut the date down to a quick chat over coffee somewhere. There will be less time to sit and fidget, and once you have finished your coffee, you can say good-bye. When you know in advance that this is the limit of the commitment, you may find that you begin to relax, and you may even decide to try to extend the meeting after all.

If you are just not on the same wavelength as your date and the going is getting heavy, it would be better to endure it with composure and leave politely at the first opportunity—declining any requests for an extension.

While humor is a great catalyst, it should never be at your own expense on a date. Self-deprecation is not worth the discomfort in trying to impress your date. Focus on your positive aspects instead.

If the date goes badly, you need to find a way to exit gracefully. You might even arrange for someone to call you at a prearranged time to give you an opportunity to leave early. You don't have to use it if it isn't needed. Don't punish yourself if things did not go as well as you expected. Instead, congratulate yourself for enduring it. Learn from any mistakes but stay positive and optimistic. A mismatch cannot be your entire fault. Talk it over with a friend and lighten the burden if it is still bothering you. You might even begin to see the funny side of it.

When it comes to turning someone down who wants a second date, honesty and kindness are a good combination: "You seem like a wonderful person, but you're just not for me."

You don't have to leave it there if, on later reflection, you decide otherwise.

Dating is not an exact science. There is bound to be someone else out there, even if it takes a few more tries. The task is to find that almost perfect match, if there is one. So now let us look at another real-life example of two people who successfully found each other through Internet dating.

Both Duane and Barbara had been trying Internet dating—with little success. It was amazing to them how many unscrupulous and dishonest people one can meet. Some had stretched their profiles a bit or had pictures of themselves from ten years ago. In any case, despite that, one does meet some interesting individuals.

Duane and Barbara were both at the end of their subscriptions with an online Internet service and had decided that, after their subscriptions ended, they were going to try something different. Barbara had mentioned in her profile that she would look at potential candidates within twenty-five miles of where she lived. Duane's profile was the same. With about one week left on her subscription, Barbara decided to extend her search to thirty-five miles, and lo and behold, Duane appeared. He was living about twenty-eight miles from her at the time.

She enjoyed reading his profile, but his picture showed him on a Harley. She had always steered away from bikes and people that rode them. She didn't know why; she supposed it was just a phobia. However, she found his profile intriguing otherwise. He sounded like a well-adjusted man without baggage. He asked a few questions. In her contact with him, she answered those questions. Then she asked him how he would answer his own questions. That took him by surprise. He said that no one else had turned his own questions on him before.

They struck up a conversation on the Internet and e-mailed back and forth for a few weeks. They both had busy schedules and never contacted each other by telephone. Barbara was always reluctant to release her telephone number to someone prior to meeting him. After about six weeks, they were finally able to mesh their schedules and find a time to meet in person.

On the morning of their meeting, Barbara remembers getting ready and thinking, *What am I doing? Here I go again.* Then she said to herself, *Wrong attitude!* If nothing else, perhaps she would at least meet a new friend today. *I must stay positive,* she thought.

Their first meeting was on the spring equinox of 2005. They didn't realize it at the time, but it turned out to be an auspicious date for them. They met at a seaside restaurant in Seattle. Sitting at the bar, drinking sodas and juice, they began talking and watching the miserable rainy weather and wind outside the bar windows. There was a warmth and cheerfulness in Duane's words. One of the other rules of thumb Barbara had made when Internet dating was to drink nonalcoholic beverages, as she didn't want her mind to be clouded and to shade her perceptions of the individual on the first meeting.

They were shocked when they finally looked at a clock and realized they had been talking for four hours nonstop. As they were leaving, she was thinking that of all the men she had met via Internet dating, he was one that she definitely would like to see again. However, Duane wasn't saying anything. As they said their good-byes outside the restaurant and both started heading to their vehicles in opposite directions, she was feeling somewhat downcast. Then Duane suddenly turned toward her and said, "Hey, would you like to get together again?"

Barbara was thrilled. They met again just two nights later at a restaurant that was halfway between their respective homes. About two days later, they met yet again. It was magical. They both realized that they had each found someone special. To add to this story, Barbara had been divorced for nine years at this point. On New Year's Eve of 2005, she wrote in her journal that she was ready to start a long-term relationship and wrote down the specific characteristics that she would like to find in a mate. Just two weeks prior to that, Duane had put his order in, as he calls it. He meant that he'd asked the heavens above to help him find a mate. He too had specific qualities he was looking for in an individual.

Barbara thanks the universe for the Internet, as she doesn't know how they would have met otherwise. She also thanks the universe for listening to both Duane's "order" and her journal writing. It was true synchronicity.

Since the time they met they have been a loving couple. After one year, they physically moved in together. They went on holiday trips of discovery, visiting many places on their travels. As a result, they have now made a new life for themselves in Honduras, on the island of Roatan. They had fallen in love with it on an earlier visit. At times, they continue to be amazed at how fortunate they are to have found each other and that they are so compatible. They have worked imaginatively together in creating many successful enterprises, not only for themselves but also for their community. They just celebrated their fifth year together, and they know that they will be lifelong partners.

Chapter Twelve—The Art of Love Online

Only love lets us see normal things in an extraordinary way.

—Anonymous

Not everyone who ends up meeting the perfect match online begins by searching the Internet for dating websites. It is sometimes a matter of progression through other experiences.

The trauma of learning that the loving wife you adore—the doting mother of your children—has been shot to death on her first day at work in a new job is hard to imagine. Yet that is exactly what had happened to Ron Denney.

Ron was born in Blairsville, Georgia. He left Union County High School with the highest grades the rural school had ever awarded. His dominant father had somehow been appointed by the local congressional representative to be the rural mail carrier for his area. Years before, his father was drafted to fight in the Second World War, and he managed to escape the grueling drudgery of life on a farm in Carroll County, Georgia. It had belonged to Ron's grandfather. They grubbed a sparse living from growing peanuts, cotton, or corn. Ron's father joined the Civil Conservation Corps, which President Franklin D. Roosevelt had set up under the New Deal.

By the time he met and married Ron's mother, who lived on the other side of Blood Mountain, Ron's father had found another position as a forest ranger. Ron's mother was the second youngest of seven children and the only daughter. Her family owned a considerable amount of land, some of which was subsequently taken to form Lake Nottley. Her mother, who lived to be ninety, was believed to be three-fourths Cherokee Indian, although this was never documented. What Ron remembers is the great warmth and love this maternal grandmother had for him and his siblings.

Her family gave the young couple seven acres on which to make a home. This was where Ron spent his first eleven years as a child. Initially, it had no indoor plumbing. Ron and his older brother, Frank, were obliged to work hard while they were at home. By comparison, his sister was mollycoddled. Until she was born, his mother had wanted a daughter so desperately that for the first two years of his life, Ron was dressed in girls' clothes and his hair was left uncut. Life became much harsher for him after his sister was born.

Every day, as soon as they returned from school, the boys had to change into unwashed work clothes. They were kept busy until nightfall or later—tending the livestock and working the fields. Being younger and of slighter build than his brother, Ron had to push himself in an attempt to keep up. He sometimes worked until he dropped from exhaustion or dehydration.

Having grown up in hardship during the Great Depression, Ron's father was determined not to be at the mercy of another. He kept a tight rein on expenses and did so for the rest of his life. Consequently, the family lived frugally. When he'd returned from the war, his father was a very different man. He was plagued by nightmares of the violence he had seen and endured. There was bitterness about him. He seemed to resent the charity of his in-laws who had given him the land on which he had made his home.

Despite the many temptations in the *Sears Wish Book*, each child's only Christmas present consisted of nothing more than a brown paper bag containing an apple, an orange, and a candy bar. The monthly trip to an A&P store in Murphy, North Carolina, to spend thirty-five dollars for staples, was a major highlight in their lives. It usually ended with a special treat of two-day-old glazed donuts. Otherwise, there was little time for frills.

Because he was a rural mail carrier, Ron's father's car was always smothered in stubborn layers of red Georgia clay. Every Saturday, Ron and Frank would earn a weekly allowance of twenty-five cents for washing and cleaning it. Surprisingly, this princely sum went quite a long way in the fifties. If they hitched a ride or walked into town and back, they could stretch this meager amount to include a movie, popcorn, and a Coke.

Already overworked, Ron's tasks on the farm doubled after his father started a second job. His father supplemented his mail carrier's income by working part time in the afternoons after he had finished his mail delivery. He worked for a chicken farm, where his job was to determine the sex of the newly hatched chicks. By this time, Ron's brother, Frank, who was two and a half years older, had left home after graduating from high school. Frank was studying at a pharmacy school. He had to work part time to supplement his tuition, and he was eventually recruited permanently by his part-time employer. He never did graduate from college, but he eventually entered a lucrative career with Lockheed Georgia, from which he recently retired.

There was much for Ron to do. The cow had to be milked. Hogs and chickens had to be raised, and a calf was born every two years. Managing and slaughtering animals was part of daily life. There was a smokehouse and beehives too. Crops of peas and tomatoes were canned at a local cannery. The family consumed what they laboriously grew and raised on the farm. Few remaining staples had to be bought. Ron was even able to learn to cook at night, after the chores were done. He could make fudge and cheesecakes to sell at occasional fundraising drives at his school. Ron had never owned new clothes. He wore his brother's hand-me-downs. It was not until he was fifteen that his mother finally bought him a jacket, pants, and tie of his very own at a garage sale. It felt like a celebration.

For some years, Ron had wanted to increase his strength and put on a few pounds. He longed to be able to afford some training weights and fondly hoped they would be a surprise present one day. He had seen sets weighing 110 pounds advertised in the Sears catalogue. They cost twelve dollars. One Christmas morning, when he was in twelfth grade, he was given the usual brown paper bag, which was normally all he received, when his mother said, "Oh. I nearly forgot. There is something hidden under our bed for you."

With great excitement, he extracted the large package from its hiding place. He tore open the brown paper covering it. It was not the set of weights he had anticipated; it was just a suitcase. It was evidently time for him to leave home.

After dropping out of Georgia Tech, Ron had several minimum wage jobs. During this period, he applied to take the US Post Office employee exam. He passed. In 1964, he became a substitute clerk-carrier for the US Post Office in Atlanta. His first assignment was sorting mail in the bowels of the Federal Annex, across the street from the Union Station railway terminal, which was still in operation then. He did very well there. He was among three candidates chosen to be considered for management training. Because of what happened next, perhaps it was a blessing that he was not selected. The director of the personnel department was impressed with Ron's writing ability and general intelligence, and he invited Ron to work with him.

Meanwhile, he met Judy at a square dance. She was a cute girl. After graduating from Towns County High School, she attended a trade school at Clarkesville, Georgia, and became a beautician. She was employed as a hairdresser for a few years before obtaining a clerical job at the Kennesaw post office. Ron and Judy fell in love and were married. They subsequently had two children, Stephanie and Chris.

Ron had been promoted to a clerical job in the personnel department, where he was editor and photographer for the Atlanta post office employee newsletter, known as the *Atlanta Postmark*. He was primarily engaged in the management of the Atlanta Post Office Suggestions and Incentive Awards Program. By the age of twenty-eight, he was chosen to be the public relations official spokesman for the post office. He went back to school at night and obtained his BBA degree from Georgia State University in 1974.

Having spent ten years as the PR person, he was asked to fill a vacancy as manager of retail sales. With the help of a major top-management reorganization, he found himself on a fast track. He was offered the job of director of marketing and communication for the Oklahoma City Postal District.

Judy had remained in Georgia with their children until they finished their school year and they sold the house. She applied for a transfer from her position as a clerk in the Kennesaw post office to a similar job in or near Oklahoma City. Meanwhile, Ron was able to obtain a new home for them in Oklahoma.

Tragedy struck on Judy's first day at work in her new job at the post office in Edmond, Oklahoma. It was August 20, 1986. A disgruntled part-time letter carrier named Patrick Sherrill, who was facing possible dismissal following a troubled work history, entered the building with a gun and randomly started shooting his coworkers. He killed fourteen employees and wounded another six before turning the gun on himself and committing suicide by a shot to his forehead. Unbelievably, Judy was one of those fourteen. Ron's entire world fell apart. The love of his life had been taken from him in a single senseless moment.

This incident is believed to be the deadliest workplace shooting ever. Similar stress-related actions of this kind have occurred at other post offices. Such incidents have given rise to the expression "going postal." Between 1986 and 1997, more than forty people were killed in at least twenty incidents of workplace rage.

After its shell-shocked beginning, Ron's bereavement gradually adjusted to life without Judy. He still had his new home. Chris was still living with him, and Ron was able to concentrate on his upbringing and the career that would support it.

Before moving to Oklahoma and the tragedy that lay ahead, while Ron and Judy were both working for the postal service, they had settled near Sandy Plains Road in Marietta, Georgia. They owned a modest home in a family neighborhood with an aboveground pool in the backyard. They were a happy young family with many friends nearby. It was a good life. They went camping, dirt bike riding, and partied with their neighbors.

Even while Judy was alive, it had been difficult raising Stephanie, the eldest child, in 1984 and 1985. After she graduated from high school, Stephanie chose a boyfriend who did not impress Ron at all. He had always regarded men whose baseball cap was worn backward as being rather dumb. It did nothing to endear him toward Stephanie's boyfriend. He and Judy were therefore upset when the rebellious Stephanie came home one day to announce that she and her unpopular boyfriend had been married by a justice of the peace the previous night. Stephanie and Judy were never reconciled. To this day, it remains a matter of deep regret to Stephanie.

In July 1987, Ron had the good fortune to meet Susan while he was still living in Oklahoma City. They fell in love and were married in October of that same year. Two daughters, Jordan and Madison, were born. Meanwhile, the US Postal Service needed Ron and his team to breathe new life into their Atlanta operation. So they moved the entire team to Georgia.

In 1990, a private citizen who had observed a possible market in discounted presorted bulk mailing approached Ron. Already at the cutting edge of the industry, Ron had the technical ability and specialized knowledge to develop such an enterprise. It was perfect timing and well before the Internet's information highway encroached on the postal system. Plans were made, and after two months, Ron resigned from the United States Postal Service. He and his business partner were able to encourage many private investors to join them. The operation took off with unprecedented success.

Although his former employer also benefited, nobody there could understand why such a high-ranking executive as Ron would choose to leave the United State Postal Service. A thorough investigation followed. It lasted a whole year before it petered out. Nothing untoward had happened. All suspicions were eventually allayed.

The corporate presorting enterprise became enormously profitable. The original business plan estimated that the company would be profiting at the end of twelve months. It made this target in only four months. Its private investors could not believe the returns on their money. Companies flocked to take advantage of the state-of-the-art service that was offered. By the time Ron was ready to sell out his interest and retire, his company owned seven of the expensive computer-driven machines that were used in the process. Each machine had cost one million dollars.

Although Susan had been married three times before she'd met Ron, she had no children by any former husband. When they'd moved back to Atlanta from Oklahoma and Ron's private enterprise flourished, their lifestyle had changed dramatically. Ron, a talented and creative artist, acquired a beautiful large house in Kennesaw, which he remodeled with great imagination. He had it professionally redecorated. It epitomized the symbol of luxury that had been missing in his deprived childhood.

For almost thirteen years, his marriage to Susan had seemed ideal. These seemed to be some of the happiest, luckiest, and most affluent years of his life. It was almost miraculous. They woke up together every day, greeting each other with loving words of endearment. Each claimed a love that was greater than the other's:

"I love you," Ron would say.

"I love you more," Susan would reply.

"No, I love you more," Ron would insist.

So the loving and amusing little argument would run. Then one day, without any warning, Susan told Ron that she was going to file for divorce. He had no idea why. It was like a bolt from the blue. He was blindsided.

To settle her claim against their assets, he was forced to sell a large portion of the valuable land on which the luxurious house stood in Kennesaw. He sold nine acres and retained only two. Susan removed many of the contents as well as half his remaining net worth.

The devastation, sadness, and loss that Ron experienced during that time were immense. It culminated in the heart-wrenching moment when he had to watch his daughters leave with Susan and their belongings. It seemed an even greater burden to bear than the sudden tragedy of Judy's death. It tore his life apart. The divorce was final on November 3, 2000.

Retired and left alone in his large house, Ron took up painting again. He preferred the medium of watercolor. He missed the regular company of his daughters and the companionship of a wife.

Ron eventually decided to try online dating and registered with Match.com. He wrote a profile and submitted a photograph. No address or telephone number was necessary. In fact, neither was recommended. Contact could be established by signals known as "winks," which were simply acknowledgements. He could review the profiles submitted by women he was considering long before he "winked" or made contact with any of them. An online instant message service on the website allowed communication between people without their having to resort to personal e-mails.

As he could afford it, he dated women for the first time by taking them out to dinner. It was pleasant and civilized. Over six years, he met many women in this way, but he never dated any of them a second time. There was just no spark, no chemistry. A profile can tell you a lot, but it cannot tell you whether you will light up when you meet.

After he received a profile from Neely Cousins, he made a date with her. It was in February 2004. He got to the rendezvous early and took a seat at the bar, where he could see people as they entered. He thought he was going to be stood up, but finally Neely arrived, and he noticed her immediately. He swung around in his seat and got up to greet her. It was like magic. There was such uncanny warmth between them. It was as though they had known each other all their lives. They even hugged and kissed each other. It was an amazing first meeting. Where had this wonderful woman come from?

Neely was christened Cornelia after her father—Cornelius. She and her sister were born and raised in Yazoo City, Mississippi. Her father, who worked successfully for a chemical company, even without having a degree, was determined that his daughters would receive a good education. He made sure that they went to college at the University of Southern Mississippi and earned their degrees. Her mother and two of her aunts had an entrepreneurial flare, which Neely and her sister also shared.

Neely was employed by IBM as a systems engineer and had worked in the computer industry all her life. Neely's first husband, Chuck, was also a systems engineer. She'd met him at IBM. Sadly, she lost him when he died from a heart attack at the age of fifty-eight. Her son, Chris, was still at college. She became a self-employed contract programmer and continued in this business for many years. In her spare time, she loves to paint pictures. Her favorite medium is oils. She has been painting since Chris was a baby.

Two years after Chuck's death, Neely was still working hard. Chris graduated from college. He considered becoming a doctor. His best friend was already at medical school. However, he took a minimum wage job with a veterinarian and found out that he preferred working with animals. While he was at veterinarian school at the University of Georgia, he fell in love with Laura, who was then his teacher.

A widow living alone, Neely was invited by a widowed female friend to come to a wine tasting at a restaurant. It was there that she met a retired Delta pilot whose name was Bill. He asked her out. She was scared to death. He seemed so exotic and had so much international experience. It was exciting. When he arrived to pick her up in his big Mercedes, she began to have doubts. It had been ten years since she'd had sex. Could she even remember how? She thought to herself, *Can I really do this?*

They traveled together constantly. They were sexually compatible too. After a year or so, Bill proposed, and they were married. It was only afterward that Neely discovered that Bill had a stingy side to his nature. After their honeymoon, she was rather surprised when he presented her with an invoice for her share of their honeymoon expenses. This continued to pervade every aspect of their ménage.

The problem began when Bill developed a fanatical interest in religion. Neely had been raised attending the Methodist church. Bill had already converted to Roman Catholicism. His fanaticism started with a visit to Magigoria, where certain pilgrims have been said to experience the presence of the Virgin Mary and to smell the scent of roses when the phenomenon occurs. It is a theory heavily supported by the Catholic convents and clergy. It has become a successful commercial operation too.

It is a dismal place, but Bill met a visionary there who convinced him that he was on the brink of a phenomenal discovery. He was so impressed by the concept that he went straight into the nearest Catholic church he could find on the way home. It turned out to be a Greek Orthodox church, but Bill was quite undeterred.

The idea was so compelling to him that he became convinced that his marriage to Neely was improper in the eyes of God and should therefore be corrected by reenacting it in a Catholic church. He persuaded her that she would have to convert to Roman Catholicism in order to be remarried in a Catholic church. His visionary friend became a frequent visitor to their home. Bill found a Catholic priest in a small mountain town in North Carolina who agreed to teach Neely the catechism before eventually conducting the mass at which their Catholic marriage would take place. This involved long, mountainous car journeys back and forth. However, the proposition was basically flawed because Bill was unable to persuade the church to annul his previous marriage. Therefore, any Catholic marriage ceremony conducted for Bill and Neely in the North Carolina mountains would scarcely be a legal one in the eyes of the church.

There came a time when Bill brought home a Mexican statue of the Madonna and placed it reverently in the sitting room of their home, where it occupied a shrine-like position. When she was expecting guests one day, she asked Bill if he would move the effigy to another room to avoid having to answer embarrassing questions. He adamantly refused. This was the end as far as Neely was concerned. She had already given in too much to Bill's fanaticism, which by now was causing them great unhappiness. Inevitably, her marriage to Bill ended after another frustrating year.

She put her mistake behind her and continued to work as a contract programmer, living in a delightful lakeside house in East Cobb County. A normal life had finally returned. A younger widowed friend was a neighbor. She had also worked for IBM. She was an attractive redhead in her late forties. She mentioned that she had registered with Match.com and had started to meet some interesting men this way. She encouraged Neely to register too.

Before her first uplifting meeting with Ron, she had met three other men through Match.com. Nothing encouraging had occurred until then. Meeting Ron that February was like a breath of fresh air. He was such fun and they had so much in common—particularly their joy in painting.

Their first meeting was at a restaurant named Aspens. They talked for hours over their meal. Eventually, the manager approached them apologetically, saying that he needed their table and kindly conducted them to comfortable seats beside the fireplace. They cuddled each other there over glasses of brandy and continued talking until the place closed. Neely asked Ron if he would like to come home with her and see her paintings. They were unbelievably happy, and there was much kissing. It was love at first sight.

Ron enjoyed Neely's lakeside home, of which she was justifiably proud. On their second date, Ron invited her to his house in Kennesaw. Its magnificence took her breath away. It felt comfortable to her—even if its style was a little more ornate than she would have chosen. Her choice would have been less formal.

"What hotel is this?" she asked. She thought it was magnificent, but she said to herself, *God, this isn't me.*

Neely was quickly invited to meet Ron's family. They dated for two years, planning their future.

As they were not sure about which house they would occupy, they decided to try to sell both properties. Neely's sold quite quickly, but Ron's did not, so they decided to live in it. Besides, it continued to provide a familiar home for Ron's younger daughters, Jordan and Madison, when they visited.

They decided to marry. Neely left a telephone message for her son, Chris, saying, "Call me back. We're getting married. I am so excited!"

Neely was amazed that in her sixties, she was enjoying the best sex in her life. They traveled. They took a trip to Bermuda, where they rented a moped, drank wine, and smoked cigars. Before boarding a cruise to the Caribbean in Fort Lauderdale, they saw a ring in a jewelry store.

"Let's get an engagement ring," said Ron, buying it on the spot.

Neely's son, Chris, had already arranged to marry Laura in June 2006. So rather than steal their thunder, Neely and Ron postponed their wedding until November of that year.

They are happier now than either of them can believe. They enjoy complete compatibility, and in their comfortable retirement, they share a deep and common interest as prolific artists. A room has been converted into a bright studio that they share. They recapture the happy memories of their travels in their beautiful paintings, many of which are hanging throughout their home. The yard is a riot of colorful flowers and foliage on terraces that contain a splendid swimming pool and a koi pond. Ron's green-thumbed childhood experience enables him to grow fresh tomatoes, cucumbers, fruit, and herbs in his garden.

Once a year, they invite their fellow artists to join them in a glorious alfresco exhibition of paintings in their yard, where the power of their love spills over into the lives of others. It is certainly a place of work, but it is also a haven of inspired imagination.

Chapter Thirteen—From Cyberspace to Elvis

Love is not a matter of counting the years...

But making the years count.

—Michelle St. Amand

Life changed for Nicki in 1985, when she and her husband sold their percentage in their moving business in New York and their home in Long Island. They headed south to join forces with a good friend who had opened a business in Atlanta known as The Bagel Eatery.

Unfortunately, over the next three years, their bagel wholesale department and their new life together failed to meet their expectations. They divorced in 1988. Nicki and her two sons moved into a condominium in East Cobb County. She was single again.

Life began to blossom once more. During the late 1980s, Elan's, a thriving Atlanta nightclub and restaurant became fashionable and popular. Nicki would often rendezvous there with her female friends. Dates with men would frequently follow. Fifteen years passed in a busy social blur. By then, her sons were fully grown, and she was ready to settle down in a more permanent relationship. The longest that had endured until then had lasted one and a half years. She was getting tired of moving on.

Friends had mentioned that the Internet had become a viable means of selecting a suitable partner, and by 2003, it was developing a good reputation. She was still enjoying a busy social life with her friends, but she felt that adding a new dating opportunity would improve her prospects. It would concentrate attention one-on-one. It seemed to offer a more focused approach to finding someone interested in the long term, perhaps leaving less to chance.

After searching some of the available dating websites, she chose to register with match and jdate. The latter offers introductions between tens of thousands of Jewish singles, but many gentile single people seeking Jewish partners also use it.

Ronnie had also registered with the same two sites, but it was jdate that brought him and Nicki together. As Ronnie is a keen tennis player, he sent out a bulk e-mail mentioning his interest in the sport. It happened to be one of Nicki's interests too, and she responded to it. She was Ronnie's first date from jdate.

They dined at Dick & Harry's restaurant. It went well. He asked her if she would like to meet again.

"Call me," she said.

However, three weeks passed before he called her. She had all but given up on him by that time.

He had wanted to play the field a little longer. He had been married twice before and had two children by his first wife. They were married in 1970 and were divorced in 1977. He was then single for ten years, until he met and married his second wife in 1987. The marriage failed, and Ronnie took on the role of full time Dad for his third child, David.

Ronnie loved being single again. He dated a lot. He took twenty-four cruises and visited Las Vegas a hundred times. He played tennis several times a week and regularly played poker with his friends. He developed a good friendship with a woman who shared the car pool on David's school run. They played tennis together.

It became more serious when she suggested that they should start looking for a house together. He realized then that he would have to break it off. He tagged along, but as they began looking at properties, he wondered, *What on earth do I think I'm doing? This isn't where I want to be.*

It was sad because he valued their friendship. They were close, but the thought of love had never entered his mind. She obviously expected more from their friendship. It had to end.

He found himself contemplating the future at the age of fifty-eight. He had so much still to give to life. He was a successful, healthy entrepreneur who kept fit and had a zest for living. He needed someone nice to love and to share it. That's when he decided to sign up with match and jdate. He and Nicki shared the same opinion of jdate. It is a character-driven site by comparison.

When they made their first trip together, it was to New York. It was like going home for Nicki. Ronnie was born in Pensacola, so it was more of an adventure for him, although he had traveled to New York on many occasions. Nicki acted as his guide, and they had a wonderful time.

They soon realized how compatible they were. Including the passionate attraction between them, everything seemed to meld together so easily. He played tennis and poker, and she enjoyed working out twice during the week, socializing with her female friends regularly, and keeping in touch with her parents and children. They both liked their freedom and followed dedicated fitness regimes independently.

At Ronnie's request, they agreed to live together. Nicki was reluctant to live in Ronnie and David's bachelor pad, so Ronnie purchased a different and more suitable home for them. They have found that everything has worked very well.

Nicki's son Craig, who is twenty-nine, lives in Australia. On the long flight to Australia to attend Craig and Eve's wedding, Ronnie proposed to Nicki.

They decided to do something audacious and quite different from any of their former weddings. As Ronnie is an Elvis fan, they flew to Las Vegas and had an Elvis Presley wedding, with all the trimmings and fun. They originally traveled to Las Vegas for a big birthday party for a good friend at the Wynn Hotel and planned to get married that weekend—in the morning before the party that night. It took place on April 30 2006. A larger-than-life version of Elvis walked Nicki down the aisle. To crown their happiness, Ronnie's elder son, Scott, made a surprise appearance too.

They now have two grandchildren. In Australia, Craig and Eve have a baby son named Ash. Ronnie's son, Scott, is thirty-seven and lives in San Diego, California. He has a little daughter named Samantha. Nicki and Ronnie manage to fly out to visit the toddler twice a year. Ronnie also has an older daughter in her thirties. She spends a lot of time in India, where she teaches yoga. She is also a masseuse and treks in the Himalayas. She is currently in America, teaching at dance camps. Nicki's older son, Chris, is thirty-one and works as a radio voice-over actor.

Having finally settled comfortably and happily over the last three years, Nicki has discovered a delight in painting. She prefers working with acrylic paints. Her artwork is taking up more and more of the wall space in their beautiful home. Nicki also sells advertising space to retailers in a weekly newspaper. What might the future hold? With Ronnie nearby to inspire her, perhaps she will spend more time painting.

Dating in general these days is very different from the days when the senior generation was in its youth. In those days, people would meet at a party or through friends. Online dating is rather like having lots of friends busy searching for someone special for you to meet. Online dating success rates are actually higher now than for more conventional means.

Part Four

Serendipity

Chapter Fourteen—Friends Can Be Lovers Too

Love is a friendship set to music.

—E. Joseph Cossman

Serendipity is a propensity for making fortunate discoveries while looking for something unrelated. In fact, serendipity is a major component of scientific discoveries and inventions. It is an aptitude for making desirable discoveries by accident. The simplest way to describe serendipity is to call it a happy accident. In other words, a serendipitous event is extremely pleasant and unexpected.

Long before the Reverend Bill Stubba was ordained, he served in the US Army's Twenty-Fifth Infantry Division during the Korean War. By chance, he met another young soldier like himself in that distant land. They had come off the battle line in order to learn how to use pole climbers of the kind that linemen use. When the soldier took off his helmet, Bill noticed his serial number, which was close to his own. They came from the same area back home, yet they did not know each other.

They both left their company after dinner on Christmas Day 1952 to return to the states. A friendship between Bill and Charlie began when they were both stranded on a landing craft in Inchon Harbor on New Year's Eve on the way to their troopship.

When they finally arrived at the train station in Utica, New York, Bill will never forget his embarrassment in front of his in-laws when Charlie pulled from his luggage a sheer black negligee that Bill had purchased for his wife, Mary. He hadn't had enough room for it in his own bag.

Charlie went on to marry a beautiful redhead from their area. Her name was Eleanor, and they had a son and became family friends with Bill and Mary. Their children formed a friendship of their own, and this resulted in visits to see Charlie and Eleanor, who had moved to Connecticut. They were once there at Easter time. Charlie had hidden eggs all over the yard and had even made footprints on the roof in the light snow that had fallen. The kids had so much fun.

Later, a job transfer brought Charlie and Eleanor's family to Atlanta, Georgia. This gave Bill and Mary's family the opportunity to visit them at their home on the shores of Lake Sinclair.

On Memorial Day weekend in 1984, Charlie and Eleanor were involved in a tragic automobile accident in which Charlie died. As soon as Bill heard the sad news, he flew down to be with Eleanor and her family. Bill was privileged to take part in the funeral service, and he returned with the family to New York State for the local funeral and burial. As an ordained church minister, Bill was honored again to be asked to officiate at his friend's funeral.

Eleanor and Bill kept in touch over the many years that followed. Then, on Christmas Day in 1992, Bill's wife, Mary, died from cancer. Bill had nursed her through her short but sadly terminal illness. After a time, Bill renewed his acquaintance with his high school sweetheart, but it was not long before he found himself nursing her through cancer as well. She too died, and he was left alone once more.

Eleanor recalls a time during one of Bill's visits from New York when they took a picnic to Stone Mountain with a bottle of wine. He then said to her, "Eleanor, if you ever need anything, I'll be there for you."

After Bill had gone back to New York, Eleanor thought about what he had said. She had kissed a few frogs over the past few years. So she thought, *Why not give my friendship with Bill an opportunity to develop into a serious relationship?* However, there would no doubt be challenges living so far apart.

In due course, Bill had occasion to attend a family wedding with Eleanor. After this, they began a long-distance courtship. He traveled to Atlanta every six or seven weeks, which kept their flame alive.

Bill traveled back and forth numerous times to see Eleanor. Their deep friendship did indeed develop into a flourishing romantic relationship. However, Bill had made a commitment to stay in New York until the end of June 2005, and meanwhile, Eleanor had no desire to return to its cold winter climate.

After several years, Eleanor was facing cancer herself, and she tried to persuade Bill to leave her and find someone else. She did not want him to have to go through yet another round of cancer, this time with her. However, Bill was adamant about supporting her, and he stayed to look after her before and after her surgery. Thankfully, today she is a three-year survivor.

They were visiting relatives on Long Island who were celebrating their fiftieth wedding anniversary. While they were dancing, Bill suddenly whispered into Eleanor's ear, "Will you marry me?" It took her pleasantly by surprise.

On June 30, 2005, Bill finally retired from his ministry after thirty-seven years. On July 16 of that same year, Bill and Eleanor were married. The ceremony took place in Tompkins Chapel at the Masonic Home in Utica, New York. It is a beautiful church, surrounded with colorful stained glass windows. Its ceiling is a panoramic view of the sky, with stars and constellations that light up as a gorgeous display.

Eleanor, whose son, Robin, escorted her down the aisle and presented her for marriage, was particularly touched that her granddaughter, Christine, stood up for her that day. Her grandson, Charlie, and Bill's grandson Ben were ushers, and the duty of best man was performed by Bill's sons, Bill and Scott. Another memorable treat for Eleanor was that Bill chose to sing to her beautifully, starting with their song, "Unforgettable," continuing with "One Hand, One Heart," from the musical *West Side Story*, and ending with the Lord's Prayer.

At the reception afterward, Bill's grandchildren kept asking him, "When are you going to leave?"

He and Eleanor finally discovered the reason behind their urgent question when they reached their car. It had been liberally decorated and covered with streamers and shaving cream.

They count their blessings day by day and are grateful that God brought them together in love after more than fifty years of family friendship. Their love as friends developed into the deep, romantic love they now share as husband and wife.

They both feel that somehow Charlie and Mary are looking down upon them from heaven, saying, "What took you two so long?"

Chapter Fifteen—High School Reunion

Live your life and forget your age.

—Norman Vincent Peale

It is daunting to many people to contemplate going to a high school reunion for the first time after many years have elapsed. Some people may feel at a disadvantage. Maybe their careers did not go as well as planned. They may have grayed, gone bald, look older, or become fatter. However, their contemporaries are likely to have changed in some ways too. They may be surprised to find how well they have fared compared to their former classmates. There is nothing to fear. A reunion is just a bunch of once-familiar people with whom one might find many common interests.

Bob Bouchard had died fifteen years ago, leaving his loving wife, Gina, widowed. Gina grew up in the small Texas town of Liberty. As a young girl graduating from Liberty High School in 1957, she was known as Gina Chapman. May 2007 marked her fiftieth graduation anniversary. Nobody had planned a classmate gathering until May 2008. Gina was alerted by e-mail and phone calls. They were to assemble at a friend's farm on Friday and then dress up and head out to the country club on Saturday night.

Gina was less than excited. Since she had been single again, she had gradually taken on many responsibilities—too many, really. She had a pressing one at which she was to preside on the very Saturday morning of the planned reunion. She couldn't remember having much fun at the thirtieth high school reunion. Her classmates had then been in their late forties, when everyone was still competing for who had the most money, the biggest car, and the best body. They were also still young enough not to feel their own mortality.

After much deliberation and calls from friends, including her old classmate Gary Tissue, whom she did want to see again, she agreed to come to the picnic arranged for Saturday afternoon and to attend the country club that night.

To her surprise, she felt the love and friendship surrounding her from the moment she arrived. They were all older and a little kinder now. They were just glad to be alive, unlike many of their former classmates. She hugged, kissed, and cried.

That night, her friend Gary asked her if he could take her to the country club. They sat around eating and telling their life histories. It was a pleasant affair. Gary took Gina to her mom's house and said a friendly good-bye. He came by again the next morning, and they went to breakfast with about thirteen others. After the reunion was over, he headed back to his home in Hurst, near Fort Worth, and Gina left for Houston.

About two weeks later, he telephoned her. As a grandmother she had just returned from a babysitting visit to California. She was telling him how much she needed to take a leisurely car trip.

"I've always wanted to drive to Mount Rushmore. Would you like to go with me?" asked Gary.

Gina was shocked, although she knew by now that Gary had also been widowed a couple of years earlier. His invitation excited her. It could be quite an adventure. So she said she would like to go with him but not for another month because her granddaughter from New York City would be staying with her for the month of August.

"How about we plan to go in September, then?" suggested Gary.

They agreed that they would leave Fort Worth on September 11, despite its ominous undertones. Gary came to see Gina during August so they could make their plans. She noticed how kind he was to her granddaughter Liberty and her little dog, and she knew that he must be a good guy. It seemed a good omen when little Liberty looked up at Gary and said, "I don't have a grandfather. Would you please be my grandfather?"

He had been married for forty-five years to his wife before she had died. Like Gina, he also had two adult children and five grandchildren. Even so, she was nervous about the impending trip, especially after he'd kissed her once before she went to bed. What a kiss that was! She suddenly realized that this trip might change everything with which she had become contented and accustomed. Even the thought of it was rejuvenating.

On the first leg of their road trip, via Amarillo, they arranged to stay for a couple of nights with friends of Gina's who lived at Taos in New Mexico, not far from Santa Fe. They planned to drive up to Laramie, Wyoming, and on to Jackson Hole and Yellowstone National Park. After that, they would cross the Badlands through Cody and finally arrive at Mount Rushmore in North Dakota. It was to be a three-thousand-mile journey of adventure and breathtaking moments.

Gary, a Vietnam vet who had been a pilot in the air force for twenty-one years, was used to traveling and happier driving, while Gina was better at entertaining herself as a passenger. She brought with her up-to-date AAA guides, which described every single town they encountered and helped them select hotels and restaurants when they needed to stop to eat or rest for the night. In fact, they fell into a pattern of stopping their journey every day at about five o'clock in the afternoon, wherever they happened to be. While they were traveling, she would read to Gary from her guidebooks so that they could both understand and enjoy the origin and history of the country they were exploring. They discovered that they shared this common interest.

When recounting her story, Gina echoed a remark made by one of her friends, "When someone feels like an old shoe, you will know it's right."

There was no timetable. They did not have to be anywhere at any particular time. They could simply please themselves. By stopping each day by five, they were able to relax and enjoy a leisurely drink together before dinner. There was no hurry to start out too early the following morning either. Their romance flourished. By taking their time and spending so much of it together in the truck each day while they explored their surroundings, they were also able to explore each other thoroughly ... and in the most relaxing way. They got to know one another well. To Gina, Gary was a familiar "old shoe." There was both chemistry and compatibility between them, and it seemed like a wonderful miracle at a time in life when both had thought such feelings were long behind them.

They did not bother to book hotels because they never knew where they were going to be. But it was off-season, and children had already returned to school by then, so there were vacancies in most places. However, there was one exception. The Yellowstone Inn was always highly sought after and often fully booked for months ahead. On the off chance, Gary and Gina decided to call them the day before they expected to arrive there. They were thrilled to find that the inn could actually accommodate them. Their rustic porch outside their room gave them a direct view of the famous geyser

Old Faithful. Although the room rates were high at the inn, they discovered that the bar was federal property, and the drinks were no more than four dollars each. There was no telephone and no TV in any of the rooms. They were left quietly to commune with nature as their only entertainment. They loved it.

They chanced to stop at many different motels and hotels. One of them provided a Jacuzzi in the room, which was fun. When they finally reached Mount Rushmore, they saw that the window of their hotel room looked straight up at the floodlit monument of America's former presidents, illuminated starkly and impressively against a black velvet nighttime sky.

The large memorial statue of Chief Crazy Horse is situated little more than a twenty-minute drive from Mount Rushmore and was well worth visiting before heading homeward to Texas. The whole journey took no more than twelve days after leaving Gina's friends in Taos, but it seemed then to stretch endlessly onward—and still does so in their fond memories of that time more than a year ago.

Since then, they have been able to spend much more time together. They drove to Atlanta to visit Gina's old college roommates and to Natchez, stopping on the way to gamble. They have visited New York together, a first for Gary, where they stayed with Gina's daughter and grandchildren. They also visited Arkansas, researching Gary's family tree.

After some babysitting in the Pacific Palisades with Gina's younger California grandchildren, they are looking forward to driving to Big Sur in California in the late summer. They have already spent time with Gary's grandchild and grand dog in Hurst. They share the same former friends and even some of the same family. Gary's sister is married to Gina's uncle, so Gary's nieces are Gina's first cousins. This reduces the number of long-distance phone calls.

151

How could old age ever be boring for this lucky couple? There has never been an argument or a cross word between these two former classmates who have waited most of their lives to rekindle a friendship that has united them in love. As Gina says today, "I have never felt so alive and happy. Never give up on love."

Chapter Sixteen—Fate Lends a Hand

We can live without religion and meditation, but we cannot survive without human affection.

—HH the Dalai Lama

When one is ready to date again, one may turn to familiar friends and pastimes only to find that, to some extent, they were exclusive to their former marital state. Couples are usually less comfortable with a single survivor of a former marriage.

Either the man or the woman of the couple may feel threatened by the presence of the single survivor. It may be nothing more than a suspicion but it is often enough to change the dynamics of the relationship.

Doug and Winnie Roote owned a beach condo in Hong Kong. They met when Doug worked for Borroughs Machines and Winnie worked for a local newspaper that was covering a press conference introducing Doug as the new head of the Borroughs office in Hong Kong. He was immediately attracted to her when he saw her face in the crowd. He made a special effort to find her afterward. A romance began. They fell in love and soon married.

Later, Winnie established her own public relations company. When Borroughs Machines decided to transfer Doug to another country, he declined the appointment. In order to remain in Hong Kong, to prevent disrupting Winnie's career, he applied for a commission in the Hong Kong Police Force.

By this time, they had moved to their new home. The low-rise duplex was situated in Discovery Bay on Lantau Island. Its windows looked east, across a sandy beach and through a hot haze of humidity, toward Hong Kong Harbor and the Kowloon peninsula. Doug was subsequently appointed to the Internal Commission Against Corruption.

Michael and Olivia Habicht, neighbors who became their friends, owned a beach duplex nearby. Olivia taught the piano to pupils who traveled to her home from Hong Kong by hovercraft. This was the regular means of transport by which residents like Doug and Michael commuted to work on Hong Kong Island. The buffeting journey across the water, in a cloud of spray, took only twenty-five minutes.

With the British lease on Kowloon and the New Territories approaching the end of its one-hundred-year term in 1997, Michael, who was born in Germany, started to make plans for their retirement. In 1984, he and Olivia bought a holiday home on the south coast of Spain. They later sold and leased backed their condo on Lantau Island. He also sold his Hong Kong company to a large German corporation that continued to employ him on a renewable service contract. Finally, after he and Olivia attended the agreed handover of Hong Kong and its supporting territories to the Republic of China, they moved to Spain to enjoy their retirement. They decided to buy a beautiful lot on a mountain overlooking the Mediterranean Sea and to build their dream home there.

Sadly, Michael's beautiful Olivia, who was of Chinese origin, became ill and was diagnosed with cancer. She managed to spend only three months in their elegant new Spanish villa before insisting on continuing her fight against her disease in Singapore, where she was born. She was the daughter of a doctor who practiced there and had died earlier in her life. Despite every medical and alternative medical attempt to save her, she died there in 2000, leaving Michael a widower. With a heavy heart, he then had to return to their Spanish villa alone.

Meanwhile, Doug Roote also developed cancer while still working in Hong Kong. He was eventually forced to retire early to the home that he and Winnie had purchased in his native Scotland. Until then, they had only seen it in a photograph. He died there, leaving Winnie a widow, of Chinese origin, to continue living alone in Scotland.

She and Michael kept up the occasional correspondence that had previously occurred between both couples. Nothing else happened until some years had elapsed. Winnie had friends living in Spain who had invited her to fly out to stay with them. She had already bought her plane ticket when an emergency caused her friends to have to cancel the arrangement because they needed to be out of the country unexpectedly.

Not wishing to waste her plane ticket, she called Michael and asked him if he could accommodate her instead. He didn't hesitate. He had started to build a guest annex at his villa, and he was excited to have a friend to visit the work-in-progress. A much deeper friendship began between them, eventually bridging the gap left by their grief. Their relationship blossomed into romance.

Although Spain is not Winnie's first choice of a place to call home, she has adapted by spending two-thirds of her time with Michael there. They also enjoy traveling and cruising together. He persuaded her to sell her remote home in Scotland and buy a more convenient condo in Epsom, Surrey.

What started as a tragedy eventually turned into a blessing for which Michael gives thanks every day. He has not only found in Winnie a romantic partner from a familiar culture but an accomplished and intelligent companion who is also a superb cook. They have discovered that they share much in common. They have also been able to share the burdens of their respective health issues. Spain is a paradise for them, but for the time being, Winnie needs to get in touch with her reality every so often by returning to her condo in Surrey.

What is the definitional difference between serendipity and fate? Serendipity is good fortune or luck, and fate is a preset destination.

Part Five

Bereavement

Chapter Seventeen—Church As a Catalyst

Love cures people, both the ones who give it and the ones who receive it.

—Karl Menninger

When a person who used to be married becomes single again, for whatever reason, some adjustment is needed. In the case of bereavement, a grieving process must take place. The time required for healing will vary from one individual to another. The period of recovery will depend on many factors. Feelings of anger, regret, guilt, injustice, or even relief all have to be processed. During this time of adjustment, an individual may or may not wish to take life by the horns. A time will come when a person feels ready to begin again.

In September 1995, Linda Williams lost her husband, Don. He finally succumbed after a seven-month battle with cancer. They had been married for thirty-three years. As his favorite holiday of Thanksgiving approached that year, she was uncertain whether, in her severe sorrow, depression, and loneliness, she could go through with preparations for their usual large gathering. Family members and friends were to meet at their retirement dream house in the north Georgia mountains. Poor Don had only managed to enjoy it for the last six months of his life.

Finally, in her deep despair, Linda put a small wicker basket, pads of Post-its, and a pen out on the kitchen counter. Every time she found anything that cheered her, such as a cardinal at the bird feeder outside the kitchen window or a note or a call from a friend, she wrote it down on a pad and tossed the Post-it into the basket. That simple act and watching the Post-its pile up lifted her spirits enough to enable her to host a quiet but loving reunion with her remaining immediate family members on the traditional holiday.

Strong feelings of isolation and loss still continued, and she learned through painful experience that what the Bible teaches about a husband and wife is true. Don and Linda had become one flesh. When Don died, she physically felt the powerful tearing away of half of herself. She yearned for him intensely. She wore his jacket. She stood in his closet and tried to smell his essence. She followed white Ford Explorers that looked like his. She looked at couples of her age in the grocery store and at church and passionately envied them. Her broken heart—not a mere idiom, but a concrete reality—was a weighty reminder in her chest of what had gone from her life.

Her little basket of Post-its steadily began to fill. But because she was so extremely weary after Don's death, it was hard to get out of bed in the morning. Two things, however, were always sure to get her up and going despite her fatigue: her pets and her church. She had two little dogs, Madison, a schnauzer, and Fritz, a dachshund, who now kept her warm in bed at night. They also had to be walked.

Then there was her church, which offered a daily morning mass at nine o'clock. Cathy, her dear friend of thirty years, who providentially lived next door, had encouraged Linda to attend with her. Don and Linda had gone to daily mass for years. The continuation of this routine allowed her to join with Don spiritually at the Eucharistic celebration. She remained part of the church militant, whereas Don was now part of the church triumphant. It brought her comfort and healing. Each day, when she returned to the house from mass, she jotted down her gratitude for the Eucharist and for the compassion of her caring church friends. She added these Post-its to her basket. The names of her constant canine companions, Madison and Fritz, of course, were also often scribbled on her diminishing pads.

After a while, the morning ritual of attending mass cemented a bond between those present at the service. Over time, their acknowledging smiles and friendly greetings to each other extended to asking for each others' prayers and to engaging in more meaningful conversations. They got to know and trust each other.

One particular person who was constantly present at mass was a retired gentleman who served as right-hand man to the delightful Irish priest, Father Paddy. Charles Cattanach was the go-to man at St. Francis. He had recently acted as the church's representative, overseer, and foreman in the building of the new church, which had its inaugural mass a month after Don had died. During Don's illness, Charles had spoken to Don and Linda many times with words of comfort. He always had a consoling and calming manner. Linda found out later that Father Paddy had asked Charles to pray for them and speak to them because Charles had cared for his wife, Donna, during her illness and death from cancer only the year before. He knew from his personal experience their daily physical, emotional, and spiritual struggles.

One day during Linda's bereavement, Charles suggested a course of action to her that he had found helpful when he has going through his own bereavement. It involved visiting a monastery at Cullman, Alabama, which runs a retreat called Beginning Experience. It specializes in counseling those who have lost a spouse. Linda decided that it might be good for her to go. Charles offered to drive her there so that he could do a refresher course himself.

Her counselor told her that when his wife was alive, she had called him on the telephone to say that she was deeply depressed and felt like killing herself. In reply, he'd said, "Go ahead, then." He was thinking that she would snap out of it. When he got home, he was shocked to find her dead after hanging herself. Linda began to realize then that her own problems paled by comparison with the enormous amount of guilt that the counselor was carrying in addition to his bereavement.

Just as the first Thanksgiving after Don's death had been hard to face, the first Christmas after he died left Linda feeling particularly forlorn. Determining not to let New Year's Eve get her down, she invited her friend Cathy and family members to join her for dinner at a local mountain resort restaurant. The company and meal were excellent, but the evening reignited memories of New Year's Eves celebrated with Don and also emphasized to her that she was alone now and no longer part of a couple. After dinner, the rest of the family went back to the house, and Cathy and Linda decided to attend the midnight New Year's Eve mass at St. Francis. Once again, she found an element of peace there, and they exchanged New Year's Eve wishes with those attending. Charles Cattanach and many other friends were also there.

That first year after Don's death progressed, and Linda's basket became so full of Post-its that she had to replace it with a bigger one. While there were awful lows, like Valentine's Day, when she realized that she was no one's valentine, there were also tremendous highs, like the surprise announcement that her daughter Romi was pregnant. Romi and her husband, Brendan, had been told they were infertile. This was a particular gift because on Don's deathbed, Romi had asked her dad to petition God that she and Brendan could conceive. They all became convinced that Don was still taking care of his family from heaven.

As summer approached, Father Paddy invited members of the parish to go with him on a tour of his native Ireland in August. Cathy and Linda talked about it and decided to go. Although both had Irish ancestors, neither had ever been to Ireland, and many of their daily mass friends were going. With the first year anniversary of Don's death coming up in September, Linda decided that a trip to Ireland was just the ticket to take her mind off her bereavement. When Father Paddy and his little group of pilgrims boarded the bus at the church in Blairsville for the two-hour trip to the Atlanta airport, their mutual friend Charles Cattanach was there early to see them off. He met them at the church and made coffee for them to take along on the ride.

The trip to Ireland, a beautiful country with lovely and gracious people, turned out not to be the answer Linda had planned to assuage her grief. The principal culprit was the Irish music the bus driver played incessantly as they traveled from place to place. Repeatedly, they heard the mournful tones of "Danny Boy." It was Don's Irish mom's favorite. Don's dad, who had died when Don was only sixteen, had sung it to their only son as "Donnie Boy" throughout his childhood. Each time the woeful song commenced, memories engulfed Linda, and she dissolved into tears.

The first anniversary of Don's death arrived on September 13, 1996, and she literally took to her bed. She lost her voice, developed a virus, and could barely get out of the bed to walk the dogs. Although she had never overtly acknowledged it, she had somehow unintentionally deluded herself into thinking that if she bravely made it through the year without him, he would miraculously reappear, commend her for her valor, and they would get their old life back. Instead, the first anniversary just underscored the certainty that he was truly gone from her forever in this life. Her body responded by shutting down its immune system. During this time, it was hard to find many reasons to add to her Post-it collection. Fall loomed upon her with the bleakness and barrenness of the winter not far behind. Soon even her wonderful flower and vegetable gardens, which had resulted in many contributions to her Post-it basket, would not offer solace from her emptiness.

After a week in bed, she forced herself up to serve a volunteer stint at the St. Francis annual fall bazaar. A friend from the daily mass group had telephoned to ask for her help, and she couldn't think of a valid excuse. The friend also mentioned that a number of the daily mass attendees had decided to meet once a week in a prayer group at individual homes. They always prayed the rosary before mass every morning, so they became known informally as "Mary's People." It seemed a good idea at the time. It would force her to get out of the house. As she left to go to the festival, she dropped a Post-it of thanks in the basket for the new prayer group.

Driving into town on old Highway 76, she glanced at the little Bunker Hill store as she passed by. Charles Cattanach, her friend from church, was coming out the door. She wasn't surprised to see him looking tired and with a slight growth of beard. She knew the men at the church had been up all night assembling the bazaar site. She decided to stop and ask him if he had heard about Mary's People. He had not at that time but told her that he would join them at the prayer group. Later Charles would tell her that while he was talking to her that morning, it was as though scales fell from his eyes and he saw her for the first time as more than a friend. It would be a while before she would come to the same awareness.

The gathering of Mary's People proved to be a highlight of her week. Their little group quickly increased in number, and their friendships grew deeper. They shared, prayed, and socialized. Furthermore, they offered other opportunities and activities to each other. These were the years leading up to Y2K, for example, and there was a lot of speculation at the time whether computers could be fixed in time to adjust to the new millennium. Several of the group members belonged to a local amateur radio club, and they volunteered the club's services to teach a course for the community to prepare for any eventuality. The local high school gave its facilities for the course. Cathy and Linda both felt technologically challenged and decided to take the course. Charles Cattanach, a longtime amateur radio operator, was one of the instructors. He offered to pick Cathy and Linda up to take them to the six-week course. They accepted, and Charles became their instructor, their tutor, and their chauffer. Linda added to her Post-it basket once more when she was able to record that she had became an official amateur operator. Her call letters are KF4PUH.

Thanksgiving once again approached, and she extended an invitation to those members of the prayer group who did not plan to be with family to join the large group observing the holiday at her house. Charles Cattanach, along with many others from "Mary's People," came to be with them. Charles arrived early, and in his customary supportive way, organized the setup for the occasion. He also stayed late to help clean up. Additionally, he helped the young men in Linda's family set up the Christmas tree. Later that week, responding to her call, Charles came back and tested her tree for trouble with the lights. As it turned out, she had a hot tree and a dangerous electrical problem, which presented a significant fire hazard. Charles handled the problem yet again, and the tree was back in business.

At Christmas, she once more invited the prayer group over to share Christmas dinner, and Charles came and pitched in to help with the accompanying tasks. That Christmas Day was special for a number of reasons. During the mid-afternoon, Romi came down the stairs holding her one-month-old daughter, Mary Virginia.

"Look!" she called out. "Mary has Daddy's heart-shaped birthmark on the back of her neck!"

The baby, for which Romi had beseeched her dad to ask God, evidenced that Christmas Day a kiss on her neck from her granddaddy in heaven, a heart-shaped birthmark identical to his own. By this time, of course, the even larger basket Linda had purchased for her Post-its was indeed overflowing.

She felt that the advent of that New Year was truly a time for evaluation. She needed to move on, and she needed to make some decisions about her life. She was living in the country on twelve acres that required lots of maintenance. Her two girls and their families were two and a half hours away. Her sons were in occupations that made them subject to constant move. Paul was a Catholic priest, and Matt, in Peru at the time, had a career in the Defense Department, which had already taken him around the world. While her dear friend Cathy was next door and her precious college friend Vonnie was in Atlanta, she still had many beloved friends in Texas, where she'd grown up and gone to college at the University of Texas.

She decided to force the issue. She called Gina, her college roommate and treasured friend, who was also a widow, and asked her if she could come and spend the month of January with her in Houston. She had three goals. The first was to exchange the worst of the winter months in the cold, snowy mountains of north Georgia for the balmy winter of the Texas coast. The second was to revisit memories of the places where she and Don had lived in Texas during their early marriage. The third was to see if going home to Texas was the right thing for her. At the weekly prayer group meeting, she asked for prayers for her trip and her decision.

The next day, Charles Cattanach called and asked if he could take her to lunch before she left for Texas. She happily accepted. He came to pick her up, and they chose a lovely lodge by the lake with a mountain view in Hiawassee, Georgia. Because she was surprised and astonished by what Charles said to her that day, her recollections of that meal are vague. What she does remember is that he told her he didn't want her to move to Texas. He announced his true feelings for her. He was in love with her. It was totally unexpected. In her surprise, all she could say was that she considered him a beloved brother. Charles told her later that her response to his declaration was the worst he could have received. She still wonders how she could have been so dumb not to realize what was happening. She left for Texas totally confused. However, it was good for Linda to leave town for a while. It would give her time to sort it all out. She would be able to talk about it to a good friend in her much-loved Texas.

Afterward, Charles told her that he had called Father Paddy before their lunch to solicit his prayers for a good outcome to the lunch, hoping that she wouldn't choose to move back to Texas. Father Paddy promised to pray.

While she was in Texas, Charles called to tell her of the sudden death of the husband of one of their church friends. While she was saddened by this news she was glad to hear his voice and to hear other news of their friends in Georgia. They talked for a long time. She missed him and the north Georgia mountains.

When she returned to Georgia, there was not much time to spare before she headed to Peru to see her son Matt, who was assigned to the US Embassy there. It was scheduled to be an exciting trip, which would take her not only to Lima but all over Peru with Matt—to Machu Picchu, the Nasca Lines, and Cusco. She was excited but apprehensive since these were the uncertain days in Peru following the taking of hostages at the Japanese Embassy.

At a prayer meeting, she asked her friends to pray with her for her trip. Charles asked if he could drive her to and from the airport, and she gladly accepted. On the way down to the airport, they prayed the rosary together and talked casually. Nothing more had been said about their luncheon discussion since she'd returned from Texas.

Charles called her at Matt's house in the Miraflores section of Lima to see how she was doing. Matt was wary about the call, which Charles noticed when he spoke to him. Matt asked what was going on with this man who was calling her all the way in Peru. She told him Charles was just a good friend and prayer buddy.

The trip to Peru turned out to be amazing but also scary. Their buses broke down two nights in a row and left them stranded by the side of the road in the Andes Mountains. The general milieu of the country after years under the thumb of the dangerous Shining

Path rebels was one of gloom. She visited Matt at his office in the US Embassy and found that after it had been destroyed by a car bomb, it had been rebuilt like a fortress. When she got off the plane in Atlanta to see Charles waiting for her, she was glad to see him and glad to be home. She felt safe for the first time since she'd left.

She is not sure just why she and Charles changed from being friends to becoming a couple. At one point, he told her, he was in the shower at his house and just cried out to God for a sign of the outcome of their relationship. After he dressed that day, he sat down, as was his custom, and read the readings from the Office (the official prayers of the Catholic Church, which are required reading for all clergy, and which are read daily by many faithful Catholics). The reading for the day startled him. It began, "There was a wedding in Cana of Galilee, and Jesus and his mother were there." Charles felt as though he had received his answer.

That passage from the Gospels was read at their wedding on July 26, 1997. During the week of Easter 1999, Charles and Linda renewed their wedding vows on a trip to the Holy Land in the actual little town of Cana of Galilee, where Jesus had performed his first miracle, turning water into wine at the request of his mother, Mary.

For her, the moment when she knew that she returned Charles's love was in an ordinary setting, but no less profound. Charles had stayed after the prayer group meeting at her house to help to fix her washing machine (the man could fix anything), and he was sitting on the steps off the utility room, working on a part from the machine. His big shoulders were hunched over as he worked on the part, and suddenly it was as though she saw him just enveloped in love—hers. That was that. She knew that she returned in abundance the love that he had been showering on her.

They shared the news with their children that they planned to marry. With the exception of Matt in Peru, who approved of Charles later when he met him before the wedding, Linda's other children already knew Charles as a friend, especially Father Paul, who was her most frequent mountain visitor. In fact, her daughter Andrea invited him to be at the birthing of her fourth child, Ave Maria, six weeks before the wedding. He had the honor of holding her hospital tray as she vomited into it during labor. Charles and Andrea developed a special relationship at that moment, which has intensified over the years. Through the ultrasound technology used in his ministry he has been the first to introduce her and her family to her last six children.

In addition, Linda had already become fond of Charles's children, Donna and Charles, and his four grandchildren, whom she had come to know because of the church. While her daughter Romi quoted Doctor Laura, who recommended dating for several years before the wedding, her son, Father Paul, settled the wedding date by saying that he was available to perform the wedding service on July 26. Paul thought this day was also perfect since between Charles and Linda, they had nine grandchildren at the time, and July 26 was the Feast of Anne and Joachim, by church tradition, the grandparents of Jesus.

So it was that Father Paul came to St. Francis in Blairsville on July 26 to "marry his mother," as he told his home parish. The church was filled with friends and family, including the nine grandchildren. Cathy was Linda's matron of honor, and Father Paddy served Charles as his best man. Their two five-year-old grandsons, both named Nick—one from the Cattanach family and one from the Williams family—were their ring bearers. Linda's three-year-old granddaughter Ariana was their reluctant flower girl.

They requested no gifts, but if guests wanted to honor them, they could have masses said for the two deceased spouses, Don and Donna, or make donations to their favorite charities in their names. At the end of the ceremony, their children and grandchildren each placed a white rose in honor and remembrance of Don and Donna and the Blessed Mother in a crystal vase at the foot of the statue of the Blessed Virgin Mary.

After the wedding and reception, they all assembled back at the house. In the center of the great room, in the midst of all of the activities, was a large wicker laundry basket. It was overflowing with Post-its. The grandchildren called it "MeMe's blessings basket".

Postscript: Twelve years later, Charles and Linda Cattanach live in Big Canoe, Georgia, where they moved two years ago so that Linda could teach language arts in the boys' middle school at Pine Crest Academy, a private Catholic school attended by seven of her daughter Andrea's children. After their marriage, Linda returned to her early vocation as a teacher and taught for several years in the Union County Middle School.

Charles, who has headed the ultrasound ministry as the volunteer head for the Women's Enrichment Center in Blairsville for the last nine years, is busy Monday through Friday. He travels north Georgia as a circuit-riding sonographer to sixteen crisis pregnancy centers. Recently, he recorded his forty-eight hundredth ultrasound. They now have eighteen grandchildren.

The large laundry basket was the last of Linda's blessings baskets. There are just no baskets vast enough to handle the marvels and wonders a generous God has sent their way.

Chapter Eighteen—Good Grief

You don't marry someone you can live with — you marry the person you cannot live without.

— Unknown

This is a story about two unsuspecting people who, although they were not searching for love, came together under unusual circumstances and fell in love. A work-in-progress, it will hopefully have no end and get better and better with time.

Marianne and John were happily married and looking forward to spending the rest of their lives with their respective spouses. Marianne was married to Billy, and John was married to Linda. Both were at the "freedom" stage of their lives, where kids had been raised, college educations and weddings were over, and grandchildren had already arrived or were expected soon. Life was going along quite nicely. The dues had been paid. All the hard work of raising and providing for their familes was nearly over. Neither of these couples knew each other. All four people were looking forward to enjoying the fruits of their labors and the rest of life's journey.

Then the unthinkable happened.

December 16, 2002, and February 16, 2003, will always be remembered. Those dates dramatically and permanently altered the lives of Marianne and John beyond their worst nightmares. For it was on those dates respectively that Linda and Billy died.

Life for the devastated survivors came crashing down like a house of cards. The next few months were a blur. Numbness set in. Nothing made any sense. Life didn't seem worth living anymore, and only the responsibilities of family and work kept them going. They felt dead themselves and invisible to others. Although well-meaning people did much to support them in many ways, they were adrift from life and perpetually sad. While others might have understood this kind of grief, only the griever truly experiences its pain. At the end of each day, both of these normally buoyant people were totally alone with only their thoughts to keep them company.

It didn't end there, however. July 30, 2003, will always be remembered too. That date also dramatically and permanently altered the lives of Marianne and John. For it was on that date that they met for the first time.

They met at a bereavement group sponsored by St. Jude the Apostle Church in Sandy Springs, Georgia. Each had missed the first grief group meeting and was asked to come early to the next meeting to register. They found themselves alone with each other in a room that was made up of a circle of chairs with a box of tissues in the center. It felt like visiting the oral surgeon and uncomfortably staring at some of his tools before he started the procedure. Neither of them wanted to be there.

"Hi. My name's John."

"I'm Marianne."

Silence.

The next seven weeks were spent learning about and dealing with the process of grief. The group consisted of ten people with an excellent leader. While there were bits of conversation between Marianne and John during this time, neither seemed interested in pursuing any relationship beyond standard courtesy and politeness. One of the tenets of working through grief is to do nothing that might significantly alter your life for at least a year. There is little chance of that happening because change is a fact of life. The group meetings ended in September. Marianne and John went their separate ways.

Three months later, there was a party for the group at a member's home. Both Marianne and John were there. The guests were in a holiday mood, and everyone had a good time. During the course of the evening, however, John overheard Marianne say that she had accidentally driven her car through the back of her garage and mentioned that it might have been subconsciously intentional. John pulled her aside and told her he never wanted to hear a story like that again. Losing his friend was not an option, and he meant it.

The following is a poem written by Marianne that describes how she was feeling then:

> *I went walking in my sleep.*
>
> *Though my eyes were open,*
> *They were shrouded by the dark.*
>
> *Days were too painful for my senses,*
> *So the nights invited my company.*
>
> *I touched no one and was invisible.*
>
> *Drenched in memories,*
> *I had only a past.*

Present and future were nonexistent,
Unnecessary, and unwanted.

Yet
I was conscious of a hesitant, comforting,
Not unwelcome presence.
Noninvasive, diffident, patient;
Walking too.
I awaken tentatively.

Marianne says that she always knew subconsciously that the presence was John.

The evening of the party marked the beginning of a continuing dialogue that culminated in a lasting and loving commitment.

Throughout 2004, Marianne and John saw each other more and more and communicated via e-mail on a daily basis. As part of his exercise routine, John walked early in the morning as Marianne was driving to work. His route happened to intersect with her daily journey at a Dunkin' Donuts shop. Many funny incidents occurred during that period.

On one occasion, their first rendezvous, John was left standing on a corner in torrential rain, wearing shorts and holding a carton of doughnut holes and an umbrella, waiting to give these morsels to Marianne as she passed by at five fifty in the morning. Thinking it odd that she never appeared, he had to give up on her after thirty minutes. Surely she wasn't off sick or something. It transpired that he had discovered a quirk in Marianne's strong sense of order. To trick herself into punctuality, she purposely set all the clocks in her home up to an hour fast. So her five fifty rendezvous occurred considerably earlier than John's.

She remonstrated later, "What happened to you this morning—rain wuss?"

"Listen," said John, "You'd better have a good explanation for leaving me in the lurch."

One of John's neighborhood friends telephoned him to ask him if it was him that she had seen standing in the rain early one morning under a large umbrella.

"Would that have been a green-and-white umbrella?" asked John, who declined to go into any further detail.

In time, they began to meet daily for coffee at Dunkin' Donuts. Their first "non-date" was due to another grief group member canceling at the last minute, leaving just the two of them. They fondly refer to this by the nickname of "Plan B". During that year, they began seeing each other often. A relationship blossomed that neither thought possible. It was like being sixteen again.

They started to become more sociable, and Marianne regained some of her natural buoyancy. A party was arranged at John's home, but unbeknown to him, Marianne had mischievously planted warning notices all around his neighborhood for all to see:

"Pajama party tonight at John's house. Come along. Bring a friend."

When John eventually proposed to Marianne, she played yet another prank on him, placing notices around the streets near his home and even at the entrance to his neighborhood:

"John Curtin proposed. Miss Mare said yes."

They became engaged in New York City in June 2005. They had attended a friend's daughter's wedding and guess who caught the bouquet in the midst of the thirty-somethings frantically reaching for it. They were married in mid-2006, with a reception at Carbo's (one of their favorite haunts) and were blessed to have many family and friends in attendance.

While there were many anecdotal incidents that punctuated this time frame and facilitated the evolution of this relationship, the underpinning factor was and still is love, pure and simple. Early in the grief group, one of the members was talking about his two wives, one marriage lasting forty-plus years and the other beginning two years after the death of the first spouse. At the time, neither Marianne nor John could understand how anyone could remarry so soon after a lifetime of a happy marriage. They realized afterward how judgmental they had been—and also how wrong.

Just as people can't completely understand agonizing grief, neither can they totally understand the overwhelming joy of finding love once again. It is something that needs to be experienced in order to be validated. For Marianne and John, that overwhelming joy of loving and being loved continues everyday. It does not diminish the love that they have for their departed spouses; it illustrates the fact that love is not finite. It can be given and received more than once … and with the same intensity.

They have just celebrated another wedding anniversary. They return each year to the Ritz-Carlton and relive the day. They are blessed with three adult children and eight grandchildren. They have moved multiple households under one roof and have made a wonderful home together. From the depths of despair they have found new love, which neither of them was seeking—and neither expected ever to experience again.

It is uncommon for members of a grief group to find romance with each other. It is the first time that the organizers of this particular group have experienced such a phenomenon. In this instance, it seems that the ten people who attended comprised a more sociable mix than is usual, and the activities of the group extended beyond the regular meeting place. In fact, John introduced one other member to someone outside the group, and that has also resulted in marriage.

In this case, it could be said that good came out of grief for at least some members of this group.

Part Six

Conclusion

Chapter Nineteen—Moving On

The only things in life you regret are the risks you didn't take.

—Anonymous

W hat is it that causes some people to be noticed and others to appear almost as though they are invisible? Why is it that some people receive immediate respect on first acquaintance and others do not? Apart from a few billion dollars, what is the difference between Donald Trump and a panhandler on the streets?

It boils down largely to what we think of ourselves. Other people react to you according to how you think about yourself. After all, people will judge a book by its cover and will often judge other people by their clothes. It doesn't seem fair, but the fundamental opinion we have of ourselves is reflected in the way we appear to others. We live out those inner thoughts in a variety of unconscious choices: eye movements, gestures, mannerisms, and attitudes that we cannot conceal—no matter what clothes we choose to wear.

Body language and telepathy are basic means of animal communication, but human beings sometimes feel that they have transcended them with the power of speech and the written word.

Yet they still underlie our whole existence, sending subtle signals without our realizing it.

Consequently, if you do not think yourself worthy of being loved, befriended, or respected, other people will subconsciously believe that about you. If you feel lonely and unwanted, the very thought of that feeling will project an aura about you—almost like wearing a label: REJECT.

So how can we overcome this? It has to begin with you, doesn't it? You have to tell yourself that you find yourself attractive, lovable, and good company. Of course, we cannot easily convince ourselves without the confirmation of others, but since we cannot control what they think, it is possible that we can fool our own minds for long enough to bring about a subtle change in what we are reflecting.

They say that if you smile, the world smiles with you. It is also true that if you smile, you will actually start to feel like smiling. You will become the person that other people want for company. It has to start within you. It is like a small ember of fire that can be fanned into flames by the warm winds of others' friendship and affection.

However, we cannot expect to rely on anyone else for our own happiness. Happiness itself is an elusive and temporary state of mind, but it can pervade more of our lives if we act and think positively about ourselves. It has to be self-generated by love of ourselves and love of life in general. When thoughts of this kind are projected unconsciously, we cannot help becoming something of value to ourselves and to others.

One has to become a giver of love and not a seeker of love. It involves an unconditional giving of oneself—not necessarily by physical donations, just an awareness of others and a latent affection for them. It might even extend to random acts of kindness. In the end, others will almost certainly love a person who can do this.

Such an attitude will eventually replace preoccupation with oneself. There is no point in faking it—trying to do things for others in order to gain their love ... trading favors in the belief that you are a loving person. Those insincere thoughts will be projected too. It has to be a genuine transformation and a personal wish fulfillment.

It can begin with small steps, all leading in the same positive direction. If your loneliness is your prison, first make that prison your home—a place of comfort and recreation. Explore interests within that home and find ways of pursuing those interests outside with other people.

There are a number of ways to begin dealing with loneliness. These involve developing friendships, achieving things for yourself, or learning to feel better about yourself.

- **Constantly remind yourself that the feeling of loneliness is a temporary one that will pass in time.**

- **Make an effort to talk to someone new. It is not easy, but you need momentum, and the first step is normally the hardest but the most necessary.**

- **Put yourself in new situations where you will meet people. Engage in activities in which you have a genuine interest and meet people who share it.**

- **Join societies like church groups, social groups, workshops, clubs, and so on.**

- **Be open to others first. A closed person cannot expect other people to share their confidences.**

- **Try not to judge new people based on past relationships. Try to see each new person you meet** from a new perspective. Believe that the person has come into your life for a purpose.

- Intimate friendships usually develop gradually, as people learn to trust each other and share their inner feelings. Try not to rush into intimate friendship by sharing too much or expecting that others will.

- Lead a balanced life. Do not neglect good nutrition, exercise, and sufficient sleep. One of the main causes of depression, which leads to loneliness, is lack of those things.

- Spend time alone. It will help you value yourself by examining yourself more closely.

- Do not become a parasite. If you seek friends for compassion and sympathy, they will be there for you, but if you repeatedly burden them with your problems, it will become a nuisance to them and a strain on your friendships.

- Reflect on good memories and count your blessings.

- Platonic or casual friendships can be satisfactory and should not be excluded in favor of purely romantic relationships.

- Learn a new skill. Success in achieving something will make you feel good about yourself.

- If you are having long-term depression, it is okay to seek medical advice. It is perfectly acceptable to get a prescription. Lack of certain chemicals in the

body can be the source of depression, which can be treated easily.

It is in the nature of human beings to be sociable. The survival and the advances of the human race have depended on it. This does not imply that an individual cannot be content alone, but good things can be achieved in cooperation with others. Loneliness therefore indicates feelings of inadequacy in being alone. So it is those feelings that have to be addressed.

We must beware of wallowing in loneliness or in martyring ourselves to it.

Suffering is not a matter of pride. We must avoid the danger of accepting loneliness as the norm, becoming immune to its pain and allowing ourselves to become reclusive. A positive effort has to be made, however small, to change the way we think about ourselves—for the better.

Why not follow Ginny's example?

• **Keep on Dancing**

Our lives are a work-in-progress. Ginny's life is no exception. She is typical of many of the readers of this book.

In tenth grade, she started dating her high school sweetheart, Robert. They continued dating for seven years. After graduating from high school in 1959, they both went on to college. Robert went to Georgia Tech, and Ginny went to the University of Georgia. Ginny left college and went to work for United Airlines as a flight attendant.

They were married in 1964, after Robert graduated from college, where he was commissioned in the army and assigned a year later to the Army Corp of Engineers. They were based at Fort Bragg for fifteen months before Robert was posted to Vietnam on active service for nine months.

They have three wonderful children—Glen, Tommy, and Leigh—who, between them, have since produced nine grandchildren for Ginny and Robert. However, they have been divorced since 1978, and Ginny continued to raise the children alone.

She still works as a senior travel consultant and has done so for the last forty-one years. She is a reliable, loyal, and fun-loving friend to many people. Although she has never remarried, there have been many romantic relationships. Perhaps due to their particular timing, some were thwarted by objections from her children.

Even now, in her mid-sixties, Ginny has great reserves of energy and stamina. In her spare time, she plays tennis regularly for a tennis team in the Atlanta Lawn Tennis Association. She also belongs to a running club. This has enabled her to run competitively in nineteen consecutive Peachtree Road Races, five half marathons, and one full marathon. She also loves dancing, anywhere and anytime. She is a ballroom dancer and belongs to several dancing clubs.

Her social life is busy too. She is on the board of a popular singles club whose events are wide-ranging and adventurous. One of her most breathtaking personal adventures recently took place in Rio de Janeiro. She jumped off a mountain on a hang glider while visiting her expatriate daughter and her family there.

There is already a new love in her life. It is in the shape of a small Maltese puppy named Belle. Ginny is not opposed to having a permanent relationship if she met the right man. As she jokingly puts it, "He would need to be very special, very loving, eleven years younger than me, and rich."

Her advice to other readers of this book is this: "Enjoy the life you have now. Don't stop playing and having fun. Take regular exercise and, above all, keep on dancing."

Author's note

Some of the stories written in this book are longer than others and may appear unnecessarily so to the reader. This is because I am concerned to preserve the integrity of the information that I receive. It is important to the friends who are involved in the stories.

I therefore encourage readers who believe they have an interesting story of their own romantic experience to contact me through the web site mentioned below. It will be reviewed for possible inclusion in a sequel to this book.

www.dontevergiveuponlove.com

9 781450 292597